ONE.

**A Process for
Building Schools of
Excellence for Every One
and Everyone.**

By Stephen G. Peters, Ed.D.
& Mark Wilson, Ed.D.

Editing and Book Layout: Terry Cortese
New Learning Concepts, Inc.
Bloomington, Indiana.
Cover Graphics: Bryant Kirk White
Cover Design: Terry Cortese
Publisher: New Learning Concepts, Inc.

ISBN: 978-1-7325646-5-7

I'd like to acknowledge and say thank you to the hundreds and hundreds of dedicated, amazing people I've worked with over the years...people I'm proud to call 'teachers.' The stories I share are of the things they've done with another group I'd like to give a shout out to: the students. Thanks to all of them and the school administrators who gave me a chance to teach, coach, and lead.

My parents, Elmer and Iree Wilson, were the best teachers anyone could have ever hoped to have. My heartbeat that keeps me moving in this work and in everything in this life belongs to Lisa, Anna, and Ellen, the greatest joys I've ever known.

~ Mark

I have had the opportunity to contribute to the field of education because of the seminal work others have done before me. Thank you school leaders, teachers, and support staff for the amazing jobs you do everyday. I'm grateful for the lessons learned from you all. I'd like to thank my mom and dad for the examples they set; my wife, Angela for making me believe I can do anything I set my mind to do and her support that allows me to do this work; Jillian and Jourdan for your unconditional love and Xavier and Maya for understanding family is everything. I am in awe of seeing our children and grandchildren take their rightful places in the world, understanding the meaning of "service above self." I am grateful to have the opportunity to be a part of the greatest profession that ever was or ever will be. We are all teachers and proud to carry the torch; one generation after another.

~Stephen

Praise for *ONE.*

As school leaders, we often talk about empowering students and listening to their voices in order to allow them to help us lead our schools. In ONE. authors, Stephen Peters and Mark Wilson, bring these voices alive and more importantly, remind us that when we allow students to lead the way, great things can happen in one community. Page after page, this book not only captures your heart, it celebrates all that is great about our profession and the impact one student, one teacher, one administrator can make in one community.

Jimmy Casas, Educator, Author, Speaker, Leadership Coach

Never has the word One carried so many prolific connotations! This book is appropriately named since Peters and Wilson use the word One to characterize the consistent, continuous climate and culture of a successful school. While effectively incorporating the brain-compatible strategies of metaphor, visualization, and personal storytelling, the authors expertly outline a school's need for a plethora of practical Ones, i.e., One individualized student, One capable teacher, One influential leader, One act of dynamic learning, etc. This is definitely One book to add to your professional library.

Marcia Tate, Educator, Author, Teacher

Nothing is more critical to the success of any school than student buy-in. Until the customers (students) believe in, appreciate, and see the benefits of the service (education) the whole process is substantially diminished. Mark Wilson and Stephen Peters have blended their brilliance to deliver outside-the-box approaches, reinforcing their vision that real buy-in is always best accomplished One student at a time.

Chad Foster Best-selling author of
Teenagers Preparing for the Real World

Ever wish you had the chance to sit around a campfire for a couple of nights with two masters and soak in their wisdom with regard to lessons learned, effective acts, and vision casting? Well, here is your chance! Dr. Stephen Peters and Dr. Mark Wilson are proven relational leaders, gifted mentors, and wonderful storytellers. Their book, ONE., is an inspirational read about how to grow the impact and effectiveness of your school one student, one educator, one act, one word, and one opportunity at a time.

Leigh Colburn, Educator and Author of the Award-Winning Book,
The Wraparound Guide

One. If we could all find a way to collaborate as One in the support and development of our children and each other, our world would be on track for sustainability and greatness. Dr. Stephen Peters and Dr. Mark Wilson have come together as One to provide excellent guidance with vivid stories of how to create experiences for each of our learners that both value and expect for them to reach their dreams. This is a must read for all educators as it focuses on school community and culture building and the power of each individual in that process. Although it is not lengthy, this book took me longer to read than anticipated, as each story spurred an idea for something to tweak, change, or implement with my students and staff. Dr. Peters and Dr. Wilson continue to inspire me and others to lead with their hearts and let their "to be" list drive their "to do" list. As practitioners in the field they have influenced thousands and continue to change lives with their dedication to mentoring and developing educational leaders.

Kerensa Wing, Principal at Collins Hill High School in
Suwanee, GA
NASSP 2020 National Principal of the Year

Contents

Authors' Notes

We were supposed to write this book, together, and at this time. We met back in 2008.

Stephen was delivering the keynote for the National Association of Secondary School Principals (NASSP) gathering of all of the state principals of the year. At that event, Mark was recognized as having been named the National Principal of the Year. Stephen autographed a copy of his book, Do You Know Enough About Me to Teach Me? for Mark, and now, over a decade later, we are writing this book together.

Our friendship began then, and has continued through the years as we each have carried out our paths in education. Both born in South Carolina, we find ourselves residents of Georgia at the time of this writing. A time with great promise and a great need for people to come together as one. There are many forces working to divide and separate people from each other as we pen this book. Schools, and the value of ensuring that 'every child' gets what they need are under pressures from every angle. This is a time where educators are being called upon to do the hard work, but the heart work that the moment calls for.

It's the right time for two people, one black and one white, united behind a belief that we can build schools for every one and everyone are writing a book about how they've been part of doing it before, and how you can do it now. We are humbled by this opportunity and exhilarated about the work we can do together to help you in the critical work you're doing as an educator.

THANK YOU for whatever role you play in the work that we do together as educators.

Stephen and Mark

Foreword

KJ

Perfect timing is a rare occurence in life. It is so rare that many never get the chance to even experience it at all. The course life takes us on is not nearly as transparent as a digital clock. In my case, life was nothing near perfect; however, it was and is filled with innumerable adverse moments and obstacles. Up until my Senior year in high school, I prevailed through those moments and hindrances with a strong foundation led by my mother and my family. Her teachings guided me to be a well-rounded young man with an impressive personality and admirable character.

The stars would align, and that guidance would lead me to form a relationship with an extraordinary man. A man who had achieved an ample amount in life from degrees to awards but still possessing a desire to reach back and give back to his community. After being featured on Oprah, he served as a consultant to educators all over the world, then returned home to serve as our high school principal. This extraordinary man is none other than Dr. Stephen Peters. Our relationship could not have been formed at a better time because I was seeking inspiration; he inspired me. I sought someone who had gone through what I have and had achieved their dreams; he provided a striking similarity. I sought another mentor for my next stage in life, he provided me with a lifelong mentorship that continues to give invaluable wisdom.

Dr. Peters came into a situation at Orangeburg-Wilkinson High School (a tough school by anyone's definition) where he set the standard immediately on the first day of school. Before

Dr. Peters, my previous principals drove Toyota Camrys or Lincoln Navigators to school, but not Dr. Peters. On the first day of my senior year, I heard about the new principal pulling up at school in a SUV we'd only seen on television or in the movies. I could not believe it, so when I got time, I went to see it for myself. Coming from Orangeburg, South Carolina, we lacked exposure in life. We have never seen something like his vehicle, so I was inspired from the first day and I had not even met the man yet.

We had a mutual friend, and at football practice, I asked him to introduce me to him. On the next day, I was introduced to him, but per usual, he was very busy in his first week of being a high school principal, so the conversation was short. It was not until the first game of the year; I caught his attention. I had a breakout game where I caught five passes and three went for touchdowns. On the following Monday, we had a conversation at lunch, and this is where we started to bond. I was interested in the how, what, when, and why of his life. Unlike most people that have achieved significantly in their life, he was very willing to share his story and knowledge.

He shared the stories of his time at Hampton University, writing best- selling books, being a world-renowned speaker, and creating his own business, The Peters Group. His inspiration is so important to my success because my goals and aspirations before him were so limited to what I was exposed to. I did not think about being a writer or keynote speaker because I never knew anyone to do that. He expanded my mind and made me dream bigger. His success made me see that it was attainable and not out of reach. Throughout the year he would tell me that he eventually wanted to achieve a dream of becoming a superintendent over a school district and the very next year, he achieved that dream by becoming superintendent over Laurens County School District 55. How can you not be inspired by Dr. Peters, who I called Dr. P? He's shown me repeatedly since our relationship started my senior year that it is expected to set the bar high and not only set it high, continue to move it higher after you accomplish that goal.

I do think the reason for his successful career in public speaking, education, and business is due to him being credible and reliable. I can always count on Dr. P to continue to ascend in life and never settle. This mentality is superbly inspirational, and it is one of the biggest reasons our relationship has lasted so long. Dr. P to me is like being friends with Jay-Z because Jay-Z never settles. He is always looking for a way to get better at this thing called life. Whether it is spiritually, financially, emotionally, or socially, Dr. P is constantly trying to get better, and I value this quality the most from Dr. P!

One day early in his principalship, Dr. P wore this gold tie, and it caught everybody's attention. It was not your regular, run of the mill tie. It was like this chromed gold, honeycomb-patterned tie that made a statement. This tie was very dazzling; however, it was not symbolic at all of what Dr. P overcame in life. During one of our first talks, he told me about his humble beginnings. He shared stories of how he went to Hampton University with one pair of shoes and how he would scrap spare change to eat sometimes. These types of talks spoke volumes to me because he seemed so relatable to me and my upbringing. I saw a man that overcame all the obstacles that were placed in his way and overachieved to the point that he could have anything he wanted to.

He and I have a fondness for sports as well. I was a football star during my senior year, and he and I would conversate about who was the better athlete. Dr. P, not to be outdone, was a very good basketball player in his high school and college years. Initially, that is how he got to Hampton University on a basketball scholarship. He would even help me get a scholarship from South Carolina State University. In college, we both played with big-time players and had a similar career path in our college years. Most importantly, Dr. P and I share the same mindset and personality I would say. We are kind of the same person. He is very giving, kind, smart, and confident. His ambition is out of this world. I view myself as the same person on my journey to being able to give back one day because of my ambition and drive to provide financial opportunities to me. I am a firm believer that you attract the energy you give out and want to attract, and that led me to Dr. P and our friendship.

After my senior year of high school, our friendship could have easily gone down the drain because we did not see each other as frequently and we were both on different and new journeys. We sustained a relationship during my undergraduate years at South Carolina State through phone calls and texts. Even though it was not often that we spoke during those years it would always seem to be timely and engaging when we did. He would check up on me here and there and would tell me of new opportunities on the horizon for him. He would remind me that I was next and there was nothing that could stop or break me. These words of affirmation kept me going during the hard times of undergrad and playing college football. He would always say he is praying for me and instill in me to thank God for all the good things. Does not matter whenever we talk, he says, "Keep God First" and he would tell me how proud of me he was for just beating the odds.

The mentorship he has given me since I have met him is astronomical because he has helped make my way to the top smoother with his free game of wisdom and even his giving hand sometimes. The type of man he is and the bond we have was just recently proven. I just graduated college and moved to Houston, TX for graduate school at Texas Southern University. Within my first couple of months down here, I was searching for a job to provide for my needs, and I was having difficulty finding one. Once again right on time, I received a phone call from Dr. P for a timely checkup. While conversing, he could tell my confidence was not normally as high as it is, and he asked how everything was going. I told him my situation and within a matter of weeks, I had a job. The bond that we have created is unjustifiably one that I value and am thankful for.

Ultimately, I am glad and pleased to be a recipient of a perfect timing event taking place in my life. It is unimaginable to think that I would not only form a friendship with my high school principal of one year but maintain a bond throughout the years that have only grown stronger through successes and failures. The level of inspiration he delivered from the first meeting and continues to deliver is priceless and the impact it is having on me is overwhelming. On top of the inspiration he provides, I view him as a split image of myself because of our life similarities and ambitious mindset. He is always willing to extend his hand to help me from high school to now, the foresight he possesses is second to none and I am forever grateful for this sustained wisdom. Dr. Peters is not stopping anytime soon, so the world should brace itself for him and the impact of the many lives he has touched along the way; therefore, as Diddy once said, "Ten years from now we'll still be on top, I thought I told you that we won't stop."

~KJ, 2021

Katherine Key

My college admissions essay opened with the line – "To truly know me is to know the town that raised me." Even as an eighteen-year-old that barely took her eyes off the future, I knew I was both a product and representative of my community. While I was not conscious of it at the time, I implicitly understood that through the support of my school and community, I had developed and refined my individual identity while contributing to the collective at large.

In their book, *One*, Dr. Peters and Dr. Wilson (affectionately known as Doc at my high school) take what I only knew as a positive high school experience and put it into an operational framework for how to build a school that simultaneously holds space for every individual student while working towards building a culture of togetherness and solidarity. Their roadmap pays equal attention to creating an environment where every one and everyone can thrive.

While reading the book and reflecting on my high school experience, I realized that the culture that Doc nurtured and grew seemed so effortless at the time, but in reality was the product of continual work, always helping us navigate the space between what we as students thought we could do and what others believed we could. From this supportive environment, we were able to accomplish many large-scale projects that you will read about in this book, including successfully lobbying for a state law and writing a letter to every high school in the country.

Although the big events exemplified the heights we could go together, I believe it was the accumulation of the small moments that had the greatest impact on me and my fellow students. Whether that was Doc standing in the hallway during class changes, greeting every student by name (or in my case a nickname he christened me my freshman year that I still use to this day), or his championing of school plays, football and basketball games, and quiz bowl tournaments alike, he signaled in small and big ways that we were important and part of a team trying to build something special.

In the book, Dr. Peters and Doc write, "we were focused on who our students were becoming as people." Looking back at all the lessons I learned in high school, it's not trigonometry or the plot of Hamlet that sticks with me, but rather learning how to navigate the kind of person and someday leader that I wanted to be. My senior year I selected a team of student leaders to spearhead many of our student-led initiatives. Doc pulled me aside to tell me that the team that I had assembled did not reflect the racial and socioeconomic diversity of our school, and without a wider variety of perspectives in leadership positions, our initiatives would not be successful. With that, he taught me that once you have a seat at the table, it is your responsibility to meaningfully bring in others, and I have tried to live this principle ever since.

In my senior edition of our annual school magazine, Pursuits, I wrote about my experience at Morgan County High School and likened the school to a large, 64-color Crayola Crayon box. In the box, every crayon is a different shade, and the built-in sharpener improves the individual crayon quality. The real magic, however, is not the individual colors, but the beautiful picture they create when they come together. Ten years later, I do not know if I have a better way to describe what it is like to go to a *One* school.

Doc called me to ask me to write a forward for this book on the day of another academic milestone, my graduation from my master's program. When I told him of my accomplishment, he congratulated me and immediately asked when I was to start a Ph.D. While I do not know if more school is in my future, I know that Doc will always be there to believe in me as I look towards the next mountain to scale. It is not hyperbole to say that Doc and his leadership at Morgan County High School changed the course of my life.

I hope throughout the book you will see the love and dedication reflected in the student stories. Dr. Peters and Doc have laid out a roadmap to create the type of school where anyone and everyone can thrive, and I hope that you are successful in achieving *One*.

Katherine Key
MCHS 2011

Introduction

All students can learn.

That seemingly innocent statement can be found in nearly every school system's list of beliefs. If you are working in a school where 'all students can learn' is a deeply held value, what does your school look like? We like to start with the list of what we believe, but perhaps a better way to create it would be to ask the people of your school and system what they see in your schools, your classrooms, and your system.

Based on the experience of your students, what is that you as a school believe? According to parents, what are the things you consistently say and do? What do the faculty and staff members see as the priorities of the system, based on what they're asked to do?

It's one thing to say you believe something; it's another for your actions to consistently show that it's what you believe.

That's why an idea as simple as 'One.' requires explanation and exploration. Can you as an educator think about your work, about your school in a way that honors every one? Please understand that this book isn't about blame and shame; quite the opposite. This book is here to help guide you in your exploration of the shared beliefs of your school and system that lead to consistent actions that are conveyed to everyone in your school world. It's not a binary examination of whether you're doing 'good' or 'bad'. Rather, the thoughts in this book are to help you examine what you think and do individually and collectively. Those thoughts and actions display your values and priorities more accurately than anything that may be laminated and posted in your buildings.

A great way to consider your work is through a process of reconciliation. For example, if you say that you want your school to be a place where students enjoy learning, do your actions support that notion or do they run afoul of it? What of the school that has posters declaring "Kids are our business!" but, in the busyness of meeting requirements, fails to create space for the adults to have regular, meaningful conversations with students? What if we say all students can learn (and I'll bet that you do) but the environment we create places a greater value on grading than learning?

The schools that do the most for their students are filled with educators who continually examine what they think and do, and the outcomes of each for the purpose of continuous individual and collective growth. We've been hypnotized into a mindset of constantly having to prove our worth via ever-changing but readily-quantitative metrics. Those have their place, but if we lull ourselves into measuring our effectiveness only by those standards, we can easily miss the higher callings.

To rise above, we have to be strong enough to be vulnerable. That vulnerability allows us to honestly look at ourselves, our collective efforts, and our collective outcomes with clarity. In that clarity, we can find the path forward to meet the lofty goals we all say we believe in. Like, all students can learn. When we share our story, it's important to put our best foot forward and let others know the good work of the school. In our ongoing self-examination, we have to look at ourselves in the brightest of lights to see it all, so we can grow from it. School people often have difficulty in distinguishing between our summative reporting and our formative self-assessment for growth. Both exercises are important, for different reasons, but are different, for important reasons. One of the things we seek to do through this book is help you better operationalize both.

With that, it's our hope that you approach this book and these ideas with vulnerability and curiosity. With an honest look at how the individual and collective actions of the people of your school align with what you have determined to be your vision, your mission, your purpose and your most strongly held values. Not from a posture of seeking affirmation for what you currently do (although you may find it); but more from a search for clarity to these questions:

- Which of our students needs something we have yet to create a space for?
  - What is it they need? In what manner do they need it?
  - How does its absence affect their approach and success at learning?
  - How might providing it affect their approach and success at learning?
- At our school, how does the whole impact and influence the individual? (How does everyone affect every one?)
  - How might we best describe the relationships between people in our school and system?

- ◇ Collaborative

- ◇ Cooperative

- ◇ Competitive

- ◇ Controlling

- ◇ Combative

- ◇ Co-Existent

- ° What might you do to influence the kinds of relationships the people of your school have with each other?

  - ◇ How do the kinds of relationships the people of your school determine what is thought, said, and done within your school?

  - ◇ How might improved relationships change the thoughts, actions, and outcomes of the people of your school?

  - ◇ In what ways do the people of your school come together to work together?

At this point, you may be thinking: that is a LOT to think about from just, all students can learn!?! You'd be right! One of the reasons to write this book is to help provoke deeper thinking on your part, richer conversations between you and your colleagues, and, as Stephen says, to reflect upon and refine your work. The lives of your students, your teachers, your school and system begin to improve when you extend yourself into deeper examination—not by chewing around at the edges.

For ALL students to learn, you have to look at each. And. Every. One. That's why we should avoid beginning questions about students with 'how many?' or 'what percentage?'. A better way to begin any conversation about students starts with 'which?'. Which of our students enjoy coming to school? Which of our students retain skills and knowledge with more frequent formative assessment? Which of our students are experiencing trauma or chronic stress? Which of our students are doing good things for other people?

If you are thinking, that's great, but we don't have the human resources to individualize every single thing we do, you are both correct and have wandered exactly into the place we'd hoped you would go. See, that's also what this book is about: the power of One. The promise of every one leads to the power of everyone. You're right, you can't do it all, but you're wrong if you think WE can't do it all. Because we, Mark and Stephen, have each been privileged to work with teams that HAVE done this, at multiple locations, different settings, but all ending the same: everyone can help every one be more successful.

The ideas we share and the stories we offer as evidentiary are not something we just imagined: everything we share in this work are things we have done ourselves (as a part of great, committed teams), things we have taught other school people how to do, and things that YOU can do as well. Both of us are teachers who have been school leaders, who extensively teach and coach teachers and school leaders. We are with you, because we're one of you. (Well, two of you actually, but you get it.)

Speaking of that, we've chosen to write the book together and for it to read that way. When people co-author a book, they have a lot of choices in how to present it, but our choice comes with some reasons. This is patently a book about *coming together as one*, so we have written it in that spirit. It connects with our broader work together, which we are also doing in tandem. In a world too often filled with voices directed at each other, we've chosen to bring ours together as one for the good of schools, teachers, administrators, and really for the good of this great big community we all share.

You'll read some stories from our experiences that are uniquely either Stephen's or Mark's but we intentionally join our voices and our experiences together to share our ideas and experiences with the intent of activating you in your work, your career, and in your life as an educator. When we're sharing ideas, you'll most likely find us using "we", and when we're sharing stories, it'll be "I". We won't make a big thing about which 'I' it is because we want the book to flow smoothly for you, and to be honest, we think it really isn't as critical which of us is sharing that particular story, but that the experience be something that's valuable for *you* and pertinent to the idea of *One*.

We approach the writing of this book, the delivery of a usable framework, and the sharing of our experiences with equal parts energy and humility. Our focus throughout this work is on you, and how this can inspire and influence you so you may impact others. We are grateful to whomever bought this book for being interested in schools for every one and everyone, and we are humbled that you are here, with us, reading our ideas and stories and reflecting on how they connect with your ideas and your stories now and to come.

Stephen G. Peters
Mark D. Wilson

May, 2021

Part I. The Power of One.

Climate vs. Culture

We talk a lot about the climate and culture of the school. The terms climate (how the school feels; the temperature) and culture (those values and priorities that drive the thoughts and actions of the people of the school) are often errantly used interchangeably (they aren't the same thing). Climate and culture do, however, have a unique relationship. Often, when I'm facilitating learning on climate and culture, I'll bring Reese's Peanut Butter Cups as a visual (and as a snack for our learners!) Climate is like the delicious chocolate on the outside of the Reese's cup; culture is the nutritious peanut butter inside. (Side bar: Dark Chocolate Reese's are basically health food. ;) If your school is all climate (all chocolate), it's no Reese's cup; it's more like one of those hollow chocolate Easter bunnies. Just a frame, nothing inside. And, peanut butter by itself is a tricky thing. Just like peanut butter in a Reese's cup, culture is best wrapped in climate. If you develop your values and priorities without an environment to protect them, it's a lot like the peanut butter without the chocolate-- missing a critical part.

Now that you're hungry for more (or, just hungry), let's take another bite. I was coaching a new principal a few years ago, and asked him what he was working on. He said "climate," which was music to my ears. You have to build the conditions for success before you develop all of the elements that go inside. He kept going though. (this was screeching to my ears this time.) "Yes, I'm going to work on climate, and when that's done I'm going to move on to the real stuff."

Was happy to get a status report; was challenged by where

his thinking was. See, climate IS the real stuff (as is culture) and you never get very far if you see them as things to do. There *are* certain tasks in leading a classroom, school or system that are conquerable, but climate and culture are standing appointments on your schedule. They are not for a specific time, but require you to click the "All Day" toggle. They represent a trajectory more than a target you're going to reach.

[handwritten note in left margin: All day!]

[handwritten note: Climate and culture are tasks for all the time]

We don't build climate as a task; we contribute to it at every moment. We don't develop culture as an agenda item; instead, we shape it little-by-little by examining it, by being honest about it, and by being intentional about what we'd like it to be. As a teacher or school leader, the Reese's Cup of climate and culture are always important to the effectiveness of your classroom, of your school. Every little thing you and the other members of the classroom do contributes to the climate. As the leader (facilitator, teacher) you have a large-sized role in doing so. The culture of your classroom is also built brick-by-brick but is in a deeper layer. Climate is how we feel; culture is what we think is important. Together, they create a space for learning that influences performance and achievement.

[handwritten note in left margin: Great summary statement]

The importance of accurately knowing the condition of the climate and state of the culture of your classroom, school, and system cannot be overstated. But, those data points are often left unmeasured or only done so sparingly because they require a significant amount of time to collect. Simply said, perhaps the most important things you should measure often go *unmeasured* because they are arduous to quantify.

When we go year after year without genuine examination of climate and culture, their health in a classroom, school, or system relies on good fortune, intuitive leadership, or some other combination of factors that line up in a winning way. So, yes, you could have a good climate and a strong culture without having put the intensive work into shaping it that way, but you shouldn't count on it. In fact, it's likely that there are classrooms, schools, and systems in which those in charge believe they have a good climate and a strong culture, but not all of the members of their groups feel that way. I'm not suggesting that people don't have bad days; they do. But when considered as a whole, which of your students find the climate of your classroom, school, system to be conducive to learning? (And which don't?)

Aha. Here's the tricky part. When someone asks you "how's the climate of your classroom/school/system?", how do you answer that question? Whose experience do you begin to think about? Whose values and priorities come to mind? What if randomly, someone in search of data collection selected just one person to answer the climate/culture questions? Does it matter who they ask? Would you be willing to let that stand as *the* answer for your school or classroom? ✗ for individuals & all

In other words, when we talk about 'how's the climate', shouldn't we be asking *how's the climate for Shantrice?* Climate is important? Check. Culture matters? Double check. As we lead classrooms, schools, and systems, which of our students, teachers, parents, staff, administrators are we considering when we look at the climate? When we talk about values and priorities that drive our thoughts and actions, does everyone live within the same culture inside our classrooms, schools and systems? Are there multiple cultures? Are there different climates? Are there classrooms parents want their children to learn in and others they want to keep them out of? (Do you get requests from parents for their children to be in/ out of a particular teacher's room?)

There's another part to the conversation concerning climate and culture. Consistency. In its absence, you lead a multiverse of climates under the same roof, the same system. With consistency, however, the climate and culture you seek can grow, exponentially.

This is what *One.* is about. Helping you to examine yourself, your classroom, your school, your system. Your climate. Her climate. His culture. Your culture.

- What does school feel like for each one?

- What are the values and priorities that are driving each one toward their thoughts and actions?

- How do we arrange our classroom/school/ system in a way that each one feels a part and believes they can be successful?

To create a school-wide climate, we have to look at the perceptions of that climate from each one. The beliefs and priorities of a school/system can't be determined in a once-every-five-years accreditation process. For the sake of consistency, value examination is something we do

6

continuously, not for compliance, but in pursuit of developing conditions that will lead to successful outcomes for every one.

We are privileged to take you on an examination of what 'One' is all about. It's through your attention to every one that you can build the classroom/school/system you want to build. It requires that you listen more than you talk. That you hear to understand and not to reply. That you do things that make every single person in your school family find their place in your school universe. That you celebrate each person for their contributions, their uniqueness, their efforts, their achievements.

Listen

You build a classroom/school/system for *everyone* by building it for *every one*. And you do that by allocating your time to:

1. listen (to students, teachers, and parents);

1. discuss and refine your school's core values (individually and in groups);

1. lead meaningful learning (in classrooms and as a school);

    2. celebrate achievement regularly. (little ways and big ways)

Build a classroom/school/system for everyone by building it for every one.

One Student

The idea of 'One.' is a two-sided coin. Equal parts. On one side, it represents the collective and means *we all come together as one.* We'll explore that powerful idea later in the book. The other side represents the individual and is based on the idea that *every single one* is important and deserves to be valued, respected, and listened to. It's in this first half of the book that we share frameworks, ideas, and stories to help you figure out how to create a space in your classroom, school, or system where every one has a place to learn, to grow, and to accomplish.

This chapter explores *One Student.* We'll share what happens when the adults in the school intentionally create opportunities for each student based on their interests and their potential. When you collectively believe that every student is of equal importance, the way your classroom/school/system operates becomes different than it was before. It gets that way over time when you consistently reflect upon and question your own practices. For example, when you celebrate the athletic team that made it to the state finals, do you also, as proudly, lift up the students on the FFA Livestock Judging Team who won their state championship? If you're a principal, you show your priorities through your calendar. Do you attend the Art Show as well as the Basketball game? JROTC Drill Competition as well as One Act Play performances?

The concept of 'One.' isn't uniformity. It's the idea that *for school to be successful for more individuals, schools need*

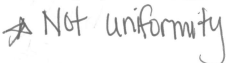

Not uniformity

forces against

to be more individualized. We have a lot of forces that work against individualized schooling: standardized tests, standardized course and curricula requirements for students regardless of their interests, and even scripted lesson plans and lessons teachers are required to use in their classrooms. As Stephen often says, school isn't broken; it's doing exactly what it's designed to do. The problem is that *it's not designed for every one,* yet we insist that everyone attend.

Dr. Ron Edmonds said in the mid-1970's: "We can, whenever and wherever we choose, successfully teach all children whose schooling is of interest to us. We already know more than we need to do this. Whether we do it or not must finally depend on how we feel about the fact that we have not done it so far."

While most of us, unfortunately, don't have all of the autonomy or resources necessary to do *everything* that each student needs, we do have enough capacity to do better for more of our students than we're doing. To do so may require a mindshift for you or for others in your school. We can do a lot to make school an individualized experience for students when the adults of the school see the possibilities of *each* student and are part of a larger effort to use that as the basis for their school experience.

Sometimes those possibilities are wrapped in a lot of layers. Here's where our collective approach makes it easier for us individually. 'One' isn't just about the one who has it figured out, who has resources for success, who always says 'thank you,' who always gives you their best effort. The notion of reaching out to 'every one' is hard! It requires us to be faithful to the work we're doing: we can't be thrown off stride from our ongoing efforts to create conditions for every one's success. It also requires us to be full of faith in what we're doing. That's easier when you're in this effort with other adults. It's harder to do in isolation, but it's harder to *avoid* doing if everyone else in your school is doing it. Power in numbers? Yes, but numbers begin with one.

Begins with one

The work we do with each student doesn't only affect them, but it changes us and helps refine us in our craft. How many times have we questioned ourselves about an exchange with a student? What influenced our thinking? Do our thoughts influence our actions? Over time, we transition from one position or title to another, classroom to office, office to boardroom. Regardless, deep in our hearts we remain committed to being who we are: teachers.

There has been much discussion lately on the idea of "our why." Predictably, as teachers perform miracles every day, (especially during these unprecedented times) we believe our focus goes beyond the "why." We must also remember, along with "our why," we must answer the question of "how?" During times like these, clarity is the next best thing to certainty.

As we commit to our work and service to our children and schools, let us all be reminded that our commitment to our profession and students provides the landscape and backdrop for amazing experiences ahead. There are so many students who continue to live in our minds and hearts. Some remain in contact with us to this day. They represent our "why." They are the main reason we believe the work can be done; that we as educators have the best chance to do it. Over the years, we have met some amazing, incredible students. Writing this book gives us an opportunity to express our sincere gratitude to our students for the gifts they have given us. Those gifts have come in many forms, but all have had an enormous effect on our hearts.

Often, we hear, this is hard work, but it's also *heart work*. We have enormous respect for our profession and those in it and believe that we are members of the greatest profession in the world. A profession that gives us a chance to make a difference for many, *one student* at a time.

Jalena

Voted "Most Likely to Succeed" in her senior year in high school, Jalena stood out among the students at her school. While many of her classmates focused on being popular and accepted, she had her sights set on college and beyond. I met Jalena while serving as the principal in residence at Orangeburg -Wilkinson High School in South Carolina. "O-W" as it is affectionately referred to, is an athletic powerhouse, launching the college and NFL (National Football League) careers of many players, three of whom won Super Bowls while playing in the league. On the flip side, O-W was an academically-deficient high school, rated first in categories you want to be last in and last in areas you wish to be first. However, I was on assignment for a year because the principal who was brought in to turn things around tragically suffered a massive heart attack and passed away. The school found itself in pain and again, without hope for direction and success.

It was an opportunity to bring about change, and our goal was to rebrand the school, ultimately matching academics with athletics. As the school year approached, producers from the BBC (British Broadcasting Corporation) contacted me from London about sending a crew to America to record our experience. After the approval process, they began filming the documentary, "American High School." One of the principled subjects of the documentary was an amazing student at O-W named Jalena Jones. She was a senior who stood out for her active involvement in numerous student activities, but even more because her academic achievement matched our vision.

Jalena had a 4.56 G.P.A. and showed no signs of letting up. She was ranked first in her senior class of over 300 seniors and focused like a laser on life, on her terms. Like Jalena, we were all focused on the work. There were days we hardly remembered the crew was filming because we wanted to turn things around and, knowing the difficulty, we knew the work could only be done if everyone stepped up and did their part.

Jalena was confident in her ability to produce academic grades and success, but naturally shy around others. When I first got to know her, to get her to talk at all, I had to ask her a question... then another, then another, and then another. Like many students, it took some time and persistence to connect.

A few weeks into the school year, Jalena introduced me to her best friend, Angela. Angela was outgoing and personable, the opposite of Jalena. Whenever you saw one, you would see the other. They were inseparable and seemed to know how to navigate the perceived distractions lurking in the hallways and breezeways of O-W.

Jalena's guidance counselor, like many of the faculty and staff at O-W, was exceptional. She kept both students and administrators abreast of what was happening each grading period and she connected Jalena and I each grading period. She understood the critical importance of being positioned and ready for opportunities and led our students in this process. Since the school is historically referred to as "O-W", we decided to capitalize on this for our branding and launched the idea that O-W means "Opportunities Waiting." (more on this later)

At each of the quarterly grading periods throughout Jalena's senior year, I found her becoming more intense and reflective. One of my favorite times during the course of my day was when students came to lunch and I would sit with them while they ate. We would converse about their day, current events, upcoming school activities and anything they had on their minds. Jalena would listen intently, but only spoke if she was spoken to. Having worked with and around students for many years, I wanted to know more about Jalena's story. I wouldn't have to look far.

On the day we announced she would graduate number one in her senior class, I met her dad. A giant of a man in many respects, standing 6 ft. 5 with a deep voice, he was a very loving and supportive father in all respects. I would discover on that day that Jalena lost her mother in a domestic shooting at the age of twelve. Her uncle was charged and convicted. As I began to process the trauma this exceptional student experienced in her young life, my mind was spinning. Questions raced in my mind: *how could she go through all of this and excel in school, graduate first in her class, and function daily as though the world owed her nothing?* Her dad was her anchor, as well as an extended family support system, as well as her church family.

The next time I would see her dad was when I visited their church one Sunday morning. I wanted to be there to support Jalena as her church was honoring her accomplishments. She was happy to see me and expressed her gratitude in her quiet way. While in service that Sunday morning, I thought about so many things, mainly, how students push through trauma, deal with adversity, and find that place deep within that propels them to desire and fight for another day, another way to love life. Whatever it was that inspired Jalena was not letting up, not giving in, and was going to see her through.

Jalena and her friend Angela, along with a few other students were selected to attend a presidential primary event in Orangeburg. Everyone dressed up and was excited to attend this event. Newspapers and major television news outlets were covering the evening. At one point, I looked over and saw Jalena and Angela's expressions and realized why I became an educator. *It wasn't to teach or lead students through a book, it was to create conditions for them to write their own book.* Further, it was to create educational opportunities for students until they could create them for themselves. That evening, among all the celebrities and glamour, Jalena and Angela were able to see the big world that awaited them. They would be able to go home with a license to dream. Experiences like these expanded their horizon, sparked their interest, and propelled them to greater heights. The more they saw, the more they wanted to see.

I believe as others at O-W believed, that that spirit guiding Jalena was and to this day, is her mother. In addition, as shy as she appeared to be, she knew deep in her heart that we represented an extension of her family; that O-W, as volatile as it could be on any given day, was indeed a very special place. She was loved, honored, and respected for being who she was. After graduation, Jalena was accepted into college in Florida and majored in computer engineering. After one year, she transferred to a college in South Carolina to be closer to her aging father. She graduated with honors and is working in her field. Jalena's success is a result of an "all hands-on deck" approach that strongly believed, failure for any student is never an option. Jalena believed in herself, her environment, family, and school. More importantly, she had a vision for a brighter future knowing her mother was watching.

A focus on every one at its most genuine level means we celebrate achievement and acknowledge effort because at our core, we value people. When the adults are able to make that commitment and live that as a truth, the students (and their parents) sense it in a very real way. And when it becomes a standard in your classroom/school/system, students are able to learn, grow, and develop with the confidence that the people around them care about them and their potential. Those are the conditions in which one student—any and every one student—can be their best.

Those are the conditions that Jalena found at Orangeburg-Wilkinson where she found *Opportunities Waiting* for her, and she responded.

One Teacher

(handwritten: definition of school)

'One.' is a way of thinking about school in these terms: we come together as one in a place where every one matters. As we do, the role of each and every teacher cannot be overstated. As you've probably heard before, there are two types of employees in school systems: teachers, and people who support the work of teachers. It's really that simple. Yes, what our cafeteria workers, bus drivers and custodians do is absolutely critical. During the spring of 2020 we saw in the spotlight the heroic work they have always done. They, and every person who works in our school systems, are more impactful than their salary might show, and more critical to our schools than our appreciation often indicates. For all of the people who fall into the category of support for teachers, thank you. That category isn't to diminish your value or your efforts at all; instead it underscores the critical nature of what you do to provide the moments we have school for. Those moments of inspiration and challenge, nurturing and shaping, pushing and pulling that happen between the teacher and the learner. Nearly all we do in and around schools is in order to create optimal conditions for the teachable moment. The learning moment.

(handwritten: 2 types of employees at school)

(handwritten: Create conditions for the teachable moment)

For those who support the teachers as school and system leaders, we are always at our brightest when we approach our work from that posture. Teachers aren't widgets for us to twist and turn into efficiency. Neither are they super-human (although they often seem to be) and able to do dozens of tasks simultaneously and equally well. They're the conduits to our students' futures. They need time to prepare for teachable moments and unfettered time to deliver those moments. If not, school is a factory line and we are just passing through on a conveyor belt.

Who is the most perfect learner in your school system? Like the shark is the perfect predator, you have some perfect learning machines in your school system. Who do you think it is? The superintendent? The Middle School Principal? The Fourth Grade Teacher?

Nope. The perfect learner(s) can be found in your pre-K and Kindergarten rooms. Every day. You should go and watch.

CURIOSITY & VULNERABILITY

They are perfect learners because they bring with them to class two critical elements for learning: curiosity and vulnerability. Don't believe me? Then you haven't spent much time with 4-5 year olds lately. Curiosity? They ask everything, all the time. Vulnerable? Ask a group of kindergartners to raise their hand if they can sing. What happens? They ALL raise their hands. Who can draw? Everybody raises their hand. Dance? They not only raise their hand, but they begin dancing right then.

Try the same set of questions with fifth graders. You'll get... different responses. Eighth graders? You may have the next contestant on The Voice in your class and he may not raise his hand when asked who can sing.

This is where the One teacher arrives. She is confident, capable, and committed and creates conditions in which the students feel safe, valued, and appreciated. When you build the right conditions, learning can happen. Students can be vulnerable because the teacher has made the classroom a safe place. You can get a wrong answer because everybody does. You're taught that triumph follows struggle. Students aren't afraid to try because they have learned the relationship between failed first attempts and successful revisions. Fun fact: EVERYTHING is a Draft. (they'll let you send your tax return late too, even in a non-pandemic year.) Too often we don't operate schools like they're a place to get messy and experiment (thanks, Ms. Frizzle). We too often create conditions that are *in opposition* to what works for learning.

Not in the *One Teacher's* classroom. Students want to come there and they hate to leave because they do things that interest them. They do things that matter. They feel safe and gain confidence through trial, error, and revision. Beyond creating an environment in which students can be vulnerable, the One teacher also leads learning through curiosity. The One teacher teaches learning through her own curiosity and her own interest in learning. She makes curiosity and questioning highly valued traits among her students. She models those virtues and as her students grow as learners, so does she.

Leading is learning, and teaching is learning. Want a great question for the hiring process? *Ask the candidate what they're learning right now. Ask them what they're reading.* You can help a learner grow. Someone who already knows it all... not so much.

In a One school/system, teachers are valued for their commitment to learning, and are acknowledged in their efforts to develop conditions in which students can more readily learn. When enough teachers connect and collaborate in these efforts, it becomes easier to be the One teacher and escape the constraints of WADITW (we've always done it this way).

Mrs. Askew

Forty-seven schools.

Marti and her brother, in their adulthood, sat down to count them all up. There may have been more, but they could account for forty-seven schools that they attended through their childhood and adolescence.

Russell Rumberger, emeritus professor at the University of California, Santa Barbara has extensively researched the effects of changing schools on student performance. His conclusions, as he simply states, are that "in general, it's bad, and the more it happens the worse it is." Rumberger's studies, as well as others researching student transfers, point out that changing schools in of itself is detrimental to student performance (test scores, likelihood of graduation); even more so, frequent transfers indicate a likelihood of instability in the life of the child.

A study published in the Journal of the American Medical Association concluded that students who frequently change schools are 35% more likely to fail a grade and 77% more likely to have negative behavioral issues at school. "Frequently" was defined as four or more times before reaching middle school.

Marti did that before getting to third grade.

Attending so many schools and eventually graduating defies all of the odds. But she *did* graduate, and from a school she attended on three separate occasions. That would have never happened if it hadn't been for Mrs. Askew.

When you attend forty-seven schools, you probably are an expert in teacher evaluation, school climate, and classroom observations. Often, Marti would be brought to a new classroom during the year by the principal or counselor only to hear her new teacher, while Marti was standing there, grumble about having a new student added during the year. (Children don't always hear what you want them to hear, but they hear more than you think they do.)

Marti had some teachers who were nice to her, some who were mad that she was there, and a lot of in-between. Some took time to get to know her while others guessed she wouldn't be there for long and didn't really invest. Spending a good portion of her childhood between homelessness, living in a car, being in foster care, running away (from foster care), it was necessary for Marti to develop an instinct of who she could trust and who she shouldn't.

Out of all of the trauma and instability that Marti lived with as a child, she did have something incredibly fortunate happen for her. She was placed in the right teacher's room at the right time.

Her name was Bobbi Askew, and she was the first person to tell Marti that she was smart. She taught Marti to love reading. She gave Marti a great gift... a dream. It was because of Mrs. Askew that Marti wanted to become a teacher. Mrs. Askew always looked out for Marti, and when it was time for Mrs. Askew's first anniversary party, she invited Marti. She told Marti she needed her help, but Mrs. Askew was really just making sure that Marti had a chance to do something special.

Mrs. Askew was smart, and kind, and gave Marti the love she needed at the time and a dream to keep her going when she went to so many classrooms where the teacher didn't measure up to Mrs. Askew.

Miraculously, Marti made it through those forty-seven schools. She graduated from high school and went to college (they will loan you money) to become a teacher. After teaching for a number of years and making a difference in the lives of children, she became an assistant principal and then a principal. Marti sought to be the kind of teacher that she needed when she was younger, the kind of teacher Mrs. Askew was to her.

Fast-forward. It's Mrs. Askew's *fiftieth* anniversary party. And Marti's there. Through forty-nine years and forty-seven schools, the constant in Marti's life was Mrs. Askew. One life-changing teacher.

Mrs. Askew gave Marti yet another gift. A piece of jewelry that she wanted Marti to have. And when Marti retired, she gave that same jewelry to Ms. Cantrell... a teacher that Marti hired, but before that, a student that Marti had taught. Marti passed it on with the instructions that when Ms. Cantrell retired from teaching, *she* would pass it on... to a new teacher of her choosing.

It's probably not overstating it to say that Bobbi Askew saved Marti's life. At the very least, she bumped her in a direction that Marti continues to follow. To this day, Marti spends her energy, her time, and her resources finding students and teachers who need a little extra attention, just like her favorite teacher, Mrs. Askew, the One Teacher that made the life-changing difference for her student.

Mrs. Black ✱ teachers 3 loves

Teachers have three loves; the love of learning, the love of learners, and the love of bringing the first two together. Dressed like she was going to work at a fortune 500 company, Mrs. Black walked into our classroom and greeted us with a calm, confident smile followed by a monologue about why that school year would be special to her and us. Middle school alone can be a daunting experience, but Mrs. Black seemed to have the master plan for creating a classroom culture that made us want to be there.

True to her word, she dedicated herself every day in ways unseen to me and my classmates. Many of us found ourselves looking forward to going to school because we were in her classroom. I often say, we must help students navigate the space between what they can do and what others believe they can do. Our new teacher made us feel like we were going places and the journey was full of discovery. The transfer of a set of expectations from teacher to student is one of the most important handoffs in life. The critical nature of the work of a teacher is complex and oriented in success or failure at many levels. The scope is deepened by influences that potentially derail the train from the tracks, as teachers attempt to be all things at all times to their students ---dedicated, persistent, knowledgeable, competent, caring, and more. Evenso, we can't always help our students overcome some of the odds they face. Nevertheless, some teachers in the face of adversity continue to rise, shine, and offer hope to those who have lost it. This is one of those teachers.

Mrs. Black walked by our desks throughout class. As the year progressed she personalized the teaching and learning process by learning all of our names; not just some of the students in her class, but all of us. Many of us were also involved in sports and our games were after school and often on Saturdays. It wasn't surprising to look into the stands in the gym and see Mrs. Black sitting there. Whose book do you think I pulled out of my bookbag first when I got home from school each day? Whose homework was done every night? Time flies when you're having fun. Our school year with Mrs. Black was one of the most memorable and we all learned so much. The learning was not limited to content, it was about decisions, actions, reactions, responsibility, accountability, and more. It was as though our classroom was a one-stop shop for everything we needed or would need to be successful in life. Our teacher modeled the presence (professional dress), the delivery (articulate speech), the substance (preparation, knowledge) and vision for all to see.

Our teacher was known to leave positive notes on our desks from time to time. I liked getting them, but loved hearing her tell me how smart I was. After checking my class assignment, she would whisper, "you're so smart." I started believing her and produced report cards with back -to-back honor roll distinctions. Having a teacher who has high expectations of you inspires you to rise to those expectations. (nobody rises to low expectations).

Though Mrs. Black was supportive of my athletic and academic worlds, she was reluctant to praise my athletic talents. She

HIGH EXPECTATIONS

would come to my games, but very seldomly commented on my basketball abilities. She was more vocal about my writing ability and my "promise" as she would refer to it. After one game in which I scored my fair share of points and we won our division, I knew the next day at school would finally draw the praise for my athletic stardom from my teacher.

It didn't happen.

What she commented on was a poem I wrote the day before our big game. She said it was "beautifully written" and that she would like me to take my writing more seriously. Upon reflection and age, I now realize, Mrs. Black wasn't against my playing basketball or any sport, she just didn't want me to limit my dreams and aspirations like so many she'd seen before me. On the last day of seventh grade, I was running down the hall and she called out my name and said, "come here." Thinking I was in trouble for running in the hallway, I braced myself for seeing the disappointment on the face of my teacher. Instead, she said the following, "I don't know what the "it factor" is or how to define it to you, but I want you to know you have it." Not knowing how to respond, I said 'thank you, have a good summer' and went on my way.

Many years have come and gone since that day, but I've drawn inspiration from that conversation so many times over my life and, more specifically, as an educator working with my students. We spend an enormous amount of time with our students. Over time, we understand the importance of our connections with them. In doing so, we realize we

teach
Content vs
children

have been trained to teach content, *but must learn to teach children*. Mrs. Black's ability to teach her students, making us feel like real human beings opened the door for learning to take place. Dr. James Comer states, "in the absence of a significant relationship, no significant teaching and learning can take place." MUST HAVE A RELATIONSHIP

The significant relationships Mrs. Black developed with her students created the right conditions for many of us to become successful in our lives. Instead of becoming a professional basketball player, I've become a best-selling author. It appears my teacher thought I was smarter than I was, so I was.

One Leader

leaders are people with titles and people without them

One is about coming together as one, and, equally, the importance and value of every one. Within any classroom/school/system, the "leader" plays an important role in the "coming together" and the "valuing all" aspects of building the school environment. Within the ecosystem of a school, there are the positional leaders, whose authority comes from being hired or appointed to a particular position. Those leaders, as well as others without the position, can also gain access to impact by being relational leaders. With or without a title, students in a classroom, teachers in a school, people in a school system can yield enormous influence. Sometimes, those with influence use it in a selfless, benevolent manner which contributes to the greater good. On other occasions, influential leaders can have agendas based on self or special-group interests. How influencers choose to use their power can contribute to unifying the school or system, or lead to a constant jockeying for power among people and groups.

The leader in a *One* school/system, in order to be effective, has to do a lot of self-work before (and during) their work with others. As Stephen says, reflect and refine. Be honest with who you are and work toward improvement. Improving to look like what? The leader in a 'One' school/system doesn't utilize control as her first means of influencing the behavior of others. The more effective leader is stronger in persuasion than control, and even more skillful yet with influence. None of that is intended to sound manipulative; it's important to know that one of the school leader's first and most essential

Self-work

tasks is bringing people together around a vision. So, you have to find a way to get people to join the effort (the cause, the vision, the mission). Antoine de Saint Exupéry (author of The Little Prince) is attributed with saying this about bringing people together:

> If you want to build a ship, don't drum up the men to gather wood, divide the work, and give orders. Instead, teach them to yearn for the vast and endless sea.

Sadly, and for a lot of reasons better discussed later, much of what school leaders are tasked to do is the first part of the quotation. Gathering wood and giving orders. If you do that, you'll get what you've been getting. But, if you have the confidence, the will, the vision, the support from your supervisors, and the nerve to do it, you can ask others to join you on a journey of success. They'll want to hear about it, and while you don't have to tell them every detail, you'll want to paint a picture for them of *what can be*. Start with the people who have the greatest sight and spend lots of time with them to come together on a shared vision. Now you have some people who are ready to take this journey with you. Others notice that something is happening. Those on the journey have a little extra spark, some added energy, some "it" factor going on. You begin to add people on the journey until you have enough to really be a force, to truly make an impact. Then, the haters find somewhere they'd rather be or, they change themselves enough to be a part of the group.

That sounded really simple, and it is. But you'll need support from above (supervisors, but, yeah, *that* above is helpful too), patience and commitment, because the previous paragraph was a brief description of … a 3-5 year process. That's a big part of what the One leader does: brings people together, values each of them, and walks together with them in a journey to success.

Leadership is Influence.

Leadership is influence. These three words have shaped the philosophy and work of many leaders and they've done so for me as well. As I walked into the principal's office at Northside School many years ago, I had no idea how much Principal Robert Hahne would influence my leadership journey. I was reporting for my first, official day on the job as the newly hired assistant principal. Dr. Hahne sat relaxed in his office in the heat of summer in a golf shirt and I walked in sweating profusely in a suit, shirt, and tie. The first thing he said to me was, "we don't wear suits to work in the summertime."

Lesson number one was entered into my memory bank, and I would add countless other lessons during my time working with him. Dr. Hahne or Bob, as he liked to be called, was a "people-person." Prior to my time working as his assistant principal, I had not seen *principals* spend their time circulating around the school building. I was accustomed to the *assistant principal* being out in the building, but not the principal.

Because of that, in some instances, the assistant principal is sometimes mistaken for the principal. Not at Northside. Not with Dr. Hahne. Bob Hahne was special; he believed in every student in the building. He believed equally in the faculty and staff, and his energy led to a positive climate you could feel as soon as you entered the building.

Educationally trained at New York's Columbia Teachers College, Bob was a humble person, but a fierce and engaging leader. He was by all accounts, a visionary and everyone from the custodians to the classroom teachers knew and believed in his vision.

Often, he would remind us that it was *our* vision, and our mission was to fulfill it. Early on in my first assignment as one of his assistant principals, I watched and learned as much as possible.

On the second day of school with students, Bob introduced me to his after-school, *"get home safe"* caravan. We were committed to ensuring the safety and security of every student. As the dismissal bell sounded, we got into separate cars and rode along as students walked home daily. We instituted a staggered dismissal schedule that released bus riders first, then walkers after buses cleared the campus. It was not popular at first, but highly effective in cutting down on incidents between bus riders and walkers. Our students and parents appreciated the extra effort shown by our administrative staff and school. The community was also supportive as we continued to ride along our students as they walked home from school throughout the school year, even on cold, winter afternoons.

As we drove individual cars along the streets our students walked home, the conversations alone provided another element to the education component at school. Our students revealed so much on those afternoons after school. We became more aware of the environments our students came from and how resilient they were. The time we spent with our students while ensuring their safe journey home in the afternoons became one of the favorite times of my day. Our students were grateful and began thanking us for looking out for them beyond the traditional school day. Relationships are everything, and the foundation from which all connections are made. At Northside, these relationships were sealed with trust and reciprocal respect. Undoubtedly, much of the academic success we would garner was born outside of the classroom of our school.

Northside was a school struggling to find its identity, mission, and purpose. Under Bob's leadership, we all felt inspired to bring our best stuff every day. He inspired all of us to roll up our sleeves and work as hard as we could. He was a very good example of a great leader. He told me once that he had never seen a highly effective school without a great leader. In all my years in public education, I have yet to see one either.

After leaving Northside to become principal of a larger middle school in our district, I found myself relying on the lessons Bob taught me about leadership and people, including:

- Keeping students at the center of all decisions and focus;

- Working to provide the resources and support for our teachers and staff;

- Culture is determined by which behaviors the leader (of any organization, school, or school district) is willing to tolerate;

- Be strategic and collect data. Many of Principal Hahne's initiatives were strategic and designed to bring outcomes which could be explained by visible data. He used data to demonstrate the effectiveness of the initiatives and make adjustments as needed.

In four years, we turned a failing school into an effective school. However, one of the lessons learned in this experience was a harsh one and remains in my spirit today. After being promoted to central office, I watched the same school that had turned around head into a decline. I've often been told that when a leader leaves an effective school, that school should continue to be successful if the right systems have been implemented and activated. In this case, much of the success we garnered was on the shoulders of a few dynamic personalities in our building. Administrators, teachers, and staff that students loved and would do anything for.

Unfortunately, I was one of those personalities. I was engaged in a conversation with another principal who said, "you were amazing when you were principal of that school that they shut down a few years after you left and turned into a specialty school." It hit me so hard, like a ton of bricks. In reply, I said, obviously not amazing enough to activate systems designed to sustain the success so many others worked to attain. This was one of the major leadership lessons in my career. I realized if I ever had another opportunity, I would get it right. And, I did have another opportunity and we got it right.

One leader can make a difference. One leader makes a greater difference when he influences others to make a difference. One leader, serving humbly makes the *greatest* difference when he joins others to activate sustainable processes that last when he's no longer at the school.

After these experiences, and with a deeper understanding of systems leadership, I became a high school principal. In that post, I focused on implementing processes rather than programs that were dependent on checks and balances. Systems that were stronger than personalities, bringing others to a commitment to a shared mission and vision.

Later, I became a school district superintendent and from day one focused on how the work would get done, who would be doing it and for how long. We started an aspiring administrative academy and as superintendent, I took an active role. I knew I wouldn't be the superintendent for the rest of my life, so we began developing, training, teaching, and empowering talented individuals in our district who showed leadership promise. I am proud of the results of these intentional efforts as many of the candidates in our aspiring administrator's program became administrators who continue to do excellent work.

We can learn a lot from each other if we have the willingness to learn and grow. To this day, I can pick up the phone and call Bob Hahne. His influence propelled me and many others to believe, achieve, and succeed, not only in education, but in life. Highly effective leaders establish relationships that last a lifetime and are not limited in scope.

An old African proverb that originated in the United States, says "Each One, Teach One." This notion is designed to accomplish something far greater, but it's also true for leaders and speaks to the possibilities of our influence.

Who are you influencing today? How are you influencing them? Over time, you may come to realize that the conversation you have with a teacher matters, the advice you give a student matters, and the extra time you spend talking with a staff member matters. The culture of your school is influenced by the sum of these conversations.

The *One Leader* is the kindling, but you don't have to be the whole fire. One person can get it started; the one leader brings together others to make sure it keeps going.

Kindling → not whole fire →

One Act

In a *One* school, learning is dynamic. At the intersection of doing and knowing, we find learning. Building a classroom/school/system where everyone comes together inherently creates a platform for action. In schools that don't reach the ideals of unity and synergy, there are fewer opportunities for action. When they happen, they are limited to individuals or only certain groups. This leaves you with a campus made up of only a few actors and a slew of watchers. And, that clearly isn't the kind of school that reaches every one.

> *We hope that these re-visits to the concept of One each chapter help to deepen your understanding of the yin/yang of the collective/individual, the everyone and every one. At a glance they seem like two different things but they really are sides of the same coin. When you get the collective portion of your school/system wrong, it has a negative impact on the individual part as well.*

What works more effectively for individuals are opportunities to activate knowledge into action. To genuinely put our learning on display. To bring relevance for what we've learned. For our learning to culminate in some sort of product:

- A proposal, for action towards a cause or improving a local or global condition;
- A production, engaging others and demonstrating depth of knowledge;

- A paper, scholarly in nature to contribute to the study of a field;

- A process, used for continued learning;

- A presentation for others, used for raising awareness or gaining support for an idea;

- A product, like a piece of art, music, writing, used to express our learning and inspire others in the same area.

If you are a student in a school where the principles of One are in place, you become accustomed to demonstrating your learning through doing, through acting. If it's a part of what you do collectively, it becomes safer to do on an individual level. The opposite is true too. Schools and systems that stop short with learning... and contain it at the recall level limit the opportunities for their students to combine knowing and doing... they stop their students short of action, and in doing so sell short the opportunity that school might afford for students. Where better to try things than in a safe place where you are valued unconditionally? Where you can gain confidence in yourself by trying, falling, and getting back up again? Building a safe, nurturing environment is not an end to itself, but rather an establishment of conditions in which students can learn experimentally and experientially. School can be these things! Don't you want a child you love to go to a school like that? Don't you want to work in a school like that? What holds us back?

Schools don't just arrive at the level of action. It's a process that takes time to build the trust and the confidence and establish the conditions in which you can have this kind of learning. In its absence, students become afraid of what other people are going to think. They can worry about what happens if they sound foolish; they also can worry about what happens if they sound smart. When we build a place where we value people and seek wisdom as a virtue, we are creating a space where learning is less constricted. We know that we've built such a place when we can see learning in action.

Here's the great thing about having a One school where action is considered part of learning: it becomes contagious. When you get that satisfaction of having accomplished something, you want to do it again. When you help someone as a teacher or a peer, you like the way that feels too and want to repeat it. Good goes around and around. Action brings on more action. Step by step you develop a setting in which your students shift from being passive into a dynamic, energetic place where students and teachers come together to do serious work in a joyful manner.

Here's a quick assessment for you to find out where you are. In a short Google form, ask your students their answer to this question:

Which of the following best describes how you see your relationship with school, and the adults at the school?

1. School is something the adults here are doing TO me;

2. School is something the adults here are doing FOR me;

[handwritten margin notes: Not seen as a one school; have 2 or 3 teacher that care about them]

3. School is something the adults here are doing WITH me.

What do you think your students would say? If they pick number one above, it suggests they don't see your school as a One school. (They haven't developed the belief they are a part of the collective, and they don't see what's happening to them on the individual level) If you have a large percentage of your students pick 1, you are reading the right book! (And you would be well served to begin planning what you'll do to change that)

What's indicated by students who select number two are those who have a positive connection with at least one adult at the school, or are people who see school as a utility or a tool for something they want. Both of those are FAR better than door number one. We definitely want our students to see school as a place where the adults want good things for them. The other side of this can indicate the passivity referenced earlier. If students feel like the adults don't challenge them, they'll pick this option.

Obviously, you'd like to think that your students would pick number three. That indicates that they see your efforts to include and engage them. They see themselves as a part of something, but in a positive way. And, if you're thinking, hey, I don't think we're doing badly, our students just don't think about it like that! OK... so, drop some metacognition on them. TALK about what you're doing as a school. Let your students know the manner in which you are trying to operate your classroom/school/system. You know what's just downright silly? If a kiddo can tell you the name and number of a curriculum standard but doesn't know whether you're doing school to/for/with him. (HOT TAKE: that kid is having school done TO him) We only have so much time with the students. Wouldn't it be helpful to discuss the absolute nature of school with them (in an age-appropriate manner, of course)? And, if they aren't feeling it, we listen to their feedback. *Why* do they feel the relationship with school that they do? *How* could school be more relevant for them? *What* do they really want help in learning? Ask them to give us examples of when they feel school is being done to or for them... and to share the pros and cons of that. And finally, to help us create and develop the space in which we do school *with* them... together.

Here's a moment of liberation for you: you don't have to come up with all of the answers. You don't have to figure everything out. If you're the principal, your best days are when you identify a problem and ask your people what they think about it. (Side bar: If you already know what you're going to do, don't ask them to validate your thinking; they won't like that and you'll quickly arrive at Unintended Consequences Avenue.) If you're the teacher, talk to your students about the classroom environment. *What we have a part in creating, we give energy to developing and take pride in defending.* A One classroom/school/system by design is a place of action.

Caleb's Law

Students at our high school were able to seek sponsorship and eventually gain the support and votes of the Georgia Legislature to enact a law. A law that we're certain has saved lives.

Yes, that's correct. Our kids got a law passed. It has saved lives. Not referring to Youth in Government (although our students gained a lot from their experience there). Not talking about our own "Sophomore Congress" which every student in our school participates in as tenth graders. (even though that's where they *really* learned how legislation works)

I'm talking about Georgia SB 360. Passed by the Senate, the House and eventually signed by the Governor. Our students, with support from many others, literally got a law enacted in our state that has undoubtedly saved people's lives.

Talk about the power of *One Act*! An education that's built on *learning by doing* leads students to a level of confidence in which they believe they can do things. There were several *actions* that preceded the passage of the law, each of them representing *one act* that triggered other acts and did something meaningful for other people. Here's how it came about.

Caleb's Law is named after Morgan County High School graduate Caleb Sorohan. Caleb played football and baseball at MCHS, was a good student, and was always, always smiling. He was nice, he was kind, and he was a good person. He graduated in May of 2009 and was home from school for Christmas vacation when he was involved in a head-on collision that took his young life. Caleb was texting while he was driving and his vehicle crossed the yellow line. Tragic and heartbreaking today as it was then.

After Caleb's passing, our school rallied around his younger sister Alex, then a sophomore, and his even-younger brother Griffin. Alex turned her grief into action and was part of our school's effort to lobby for a law to make it illegal to text and drive in Georgia.

Our students knew *how* the process of lawmaking happens not only from reading about it, but from doing it. Amy Saylor, one of our roster-full of incredibly talented and caring teachers at MCHS, didn't take the Government classes she taught lightly. She took them to another level. Read about how a bill becomes a law? Not at MoCo! Ms. Saylor led a *year-long study* that culminated in a week's worth of Sophomore Congress. Each year, our entire Sophomore Class researched laws, created a bill book, held committee meetings, and sessions of both the House and the Senate. Our kids dressed up and debated bills that were eventually signed (or not) by the Youth Governor (someone from the *Junior* Class who had been in the legislative experience the year before.

This experience was an act, *one act* that by itself might seem less than it was, but without Amy Saylor (with the collaboration of other teachers as well) putting on Sophomore Congress, our students wouldn't have had the expertise and confidence to go to Atlanta and get a bill passed. Ms. Saylor wasn't required to put on the program. No one asked her to. She was a great teacher who decided to act and built a program of learning that worked. (Side bar: we altered our entire school schedule so Government class lasted all year long instead of one semester. *This learning activity was so rich* we changed our schedule to meet its needs.)

Amy Saylor's *one act* followed Jim Malanowski's. Jim took a group of our students to participate in Georgia's Youth in Government program. His first group had a great experience, shared it when they returned, and led to Amy Saylor's development of Sophomore Congress. (Jim's first group to statewide Youth in Government went in one minivan; four years later it took two full buses to get our kids there)

What we do doesn't live in isolation. It spreads. Whether what we do is good or bad, it spreads. Whether it's our action or our inaction, our choices lead us and those around us down different paths, based on what we choose.   OUR INFLUENCE

I can confidently say that if Jim and Amy weren't the kind of teachers they were, there wouldn't have been a Caleb's Law, at least not generated from MCHS.

But they *are* those kind of teachers, and our students *did* fight through their grief and sorrow to think of others, and get a law passed. They knew how, and then they did it.

It wasn't easy.

We lost count of how many trips our students made to Atlanta in school buses to lobby House members and Senate members for the passage of the law. Our students were focused; they didn't go there to get out of class, or to be impressed with the *real* legislators. Look, our kids had done all of this before and knew how it worked. They researched the representatives and senators and went to get the bill passed, not to be starstruck or thrown off course. John Robbins, Bill Malone, and Allen Crowley took turns driving the students the hour-each-way to the statehouse where our students lobbied sometimes, had press conferences, spoke on the steps. They did it all.

The bill was passed by both the Senate and the House, and all of the members of the Senate actually looked to the Gallery where our students were and gave *them* a standing ovation when the votes were counted.

Then. All that needed to happen to make the bill a law was for the Governor to sign it. What could keep that from happening?

Turns out, the Governor can keep that from happening. Our Governor held a press conference to say that he was reluctant to sign the law because he viewed it as "unenforceable." He threatened to let it expire without his signature. Our students were devastated.

Their frustration came from the amount of work they'd put in, from appearing on television, from making up work late nights when they returned from lobbying, from the elation of passing through both chambers to the deflation of facing a threat they hadn't counted on, nor prepared for.

The Governor, however, was not prepared for the power of

teenagers with a cause. Channel Eleven from Atlanta came out to little-old Madison to do a live broadcast of a rally our students held at the school. The rally included our students getting on social media, texts, phone calls, and any means necessary to ask people from across Georgia to phone the Governor's office to request that he sign Caleb's Law. 11 Alive was so kind as to put the phone number on the chyron for us. (Thanks, Donna Lowry!)

People from all over Georgia showered the Governor's office with phone calls, emails, and even faxes (remember them?) requesting that the bill be signed and Caleb's Law be enacted. I was in the gym with our students when I was called to the phone. It was the Governor's Office.

"Dr. Wilson?"

"Yes?"

"Listen, we know your students are very passionate about what they're doing, and the Governor wants them to know that he hears them, but we can't get any business done from all of the calls that are coming in. Can you say something to them, please?"

"I'll be glad to," I told the staffer. I hurried back to the gym to tell the kids in a shout, "You've got them right where you want them! Keep calling!!!"

The Governor's Office finally got enough calls to contact Alex Sorohan, Caleb's sister. She was invited to meet with the Governor. She and one of the other students in the effort met with the Governor, who hoped he would talk them into relenting in their efforts. Alex was respectful, but declined to stop until we made Georgia's roads safer for others. When the Governor said we couldn't stop everyone from texting, Alex reminded them that if we stopped only one family from going through what hers had, it would be worth the effort.

She left his office with little hope that he would sign the bill, but surprisingly, on June 4, 2010, he eventually signed it. A stronger leader would have invited our students, particularly Alex and her family to attend the signing; instead, we heard about it in the media.

Our students continued to support the effort to curb distracted driving as in the next school year. AT&T launched their "It Can Wait" efforts at our school, and the Governor's Office of Highway Safety (not the Governor himself) asked our students to speak about the dangers of distracted driving at schools across Georgia. Alex became a national spokesperson for the effort to make texting while driving illegal. Several states followed Georgia in passing laws against texting while driving, all of which began with 15- and 16-year-olds in a rural town in Georgia. Who wanted to honor the memory of a fallen loved one. Who wanted to spare other families from tragedy. Who wanted to save lives. Who had been prepared to do real things by learning from teachers and working with adults who seized the power to act and empowered their students to do the same.

One Word

Our school prospers when our students and teachers feel like they're a part of something, and feel like other people value them. That's a short, short version of what One is about. So, how do they feel a part of something? And, why will they feel valued?

Words.

You have often heard and probably repeated the importance of relationships in schools? If you ask educators if relationships are important for what we do in schools, you'll get a near-unanimous response. Yes. Relationships matter a lot. But... what exactly are relationships? What are we talking about when we talk about them so often?

Words.

Susan Scott, in her book Fierce Conversations, offers this idea: the conversation is the relationship.

So, what are the conversations our students have at school? Better yet, think about the conversations you have with students, if you're a teacher. Your conversations with teachers and staff if you're an administrator. What sort of things do you talk about? Yes, we are working to help our students academically and in life, so we are going to have academic conversations with them, but... are you having enough conversations to call it a relationship? Is your address to the class actually counting toward conversation?

Before you pass quietly over this notion, please reflect on this, from neuroanatomist Jill Bolte Taylor. "Although many of us may think of ourselves as thinking creatures that feel, biologically we are feeling creatures that think."

How do your words make your students feel? How do your conversations lift up (or drag down) your colleagues? As your grandmother probably told you, it's not just what you say, but it's how you say it. What impact do your words... and your approach to those conversations have on your students?

So there's your student's work, and there's your student's attitude and approach to work. Which do you think is the pathway for her success? During the COVID-19 outbreak in 2020-2021, many educators decried digital platforms and virtual learning as the villains in the absence of engagement into schoolwork on the part of many of our students. Something to take away from that might be this: in the absence of regular conversations (aka relationships) with teachers and peers, the needed ingredient for success in school was missing. It's hard to precisely quantify, but a lot of schoolwork completed in the pre-COVID days at schools can be attributed to the environment of school. The environment of school with positive modeling (of engaging into schoolwork) by peers and relationships-- conversations-- with teachers. In the days after schools were sent home for the remainder of the 2019-2020 school year, students who had positive connections with teachers were, if they had available resources, more likely to engage in work at home than those students who didn't have the same kind of relationships with their teachers.

In other words, the teachers who had developed relationships could continue to have a degree of influence on their students, even as they learned from home. The teachers who had primarily used control instead of influence to get students working in the classroom may have found challenges with the absence of the physical environment.

When we are talking about relationships, we are talking about conversations. What are those conversations like? So, is it really about one word, then? Yes. And no. If you could land one word on your students that would make them feel a part of a bigger whole while feeling appreciated on their own, we know you would do it. What would that word be? Abracadabra, maybe?

It IS about one word, but here's the trick: you don't know which one. Maybe it's more like one conversation, one phrase, one moment, but it's fair enough to have a section on one word.

We've shared with educators for years that the absolute most empowering thing you should know is that you work in a profession in which you can make a difference in someone's life in an instant! Wow. Now, here's the most terrifying thing: you don't know when.

That moment that your one word may be a turning point for a student, for a teacher is out there, but it doesn't often come with bright lights and bells ringing. It's just as likely to be on a nondescript, Tuesday afternoon in March when you didn't really have your best lesson plan on and your hair wasn't really doing it that day either.

The teachable (and learnable) moments sometimes come unexpectedly. At our best, we avail ourselves to those moments by investing in the words, the conversations, the relationships. When someone comes to you for your help, you don't know what all they've had to do to get to that point. It may be colossal to them to have geared up for that moment. If you don't rise up (despite having WAY TOO MUCH to do, and being in a profession where you perform the entire time you're at work and are asked to prepare to perform on your own, spare-time, like a hobby) that moment may pass and never come your way again. And it's that moment that you do all of those other things to get to. That moment is the strawberry jelly for all of the burnt toast you've eaten. Don't miss it.

And because we don't know when, or who, or how, our careers require an incredible amount of patience, persistence, and fortitude. Because, you have got to be there when they come to you, not necessarily the other way around.

That's the price for a ticket to the world's most impactful profession. Every other profession? They had to have a teacher to get there, don't forget. When you're up to world-changing, and life-changing business, you have to be pretty good. Sure, they don't pay you commensurate with the importance of what you do for people and for the world. You knew that coming in, though, and yet here you are. And here they are, coming to you for one word, at just the right time that may be like water to a desert-traveller to them. Be ready.

Kordel

Born into the home of a loving, single mother, 6'2" super star wide receiver for the O-W Bruins, Kordel had his eyes set on college and the NFL. One of the principled subjects in the documentary "American High School," Kordel was reluctant at first to allow his story to be told through the BBC cameras. It took a while for him to trust the process and allow the reality of his story to be told. O-W was 99% African-American and 100% free lunch with one of the highest poverty index ratings in the state. We also had a 19% special education student population. Kordel was also a member of the senior class and on pace to graduate on time. His goals included playing college football, obtaining a degree and pursuing the NFL draft. He would be the first member in his family to attend college.

When I first met Kordel, he was not one to engage. I could tell he, like many of the students at O-W, didn't trust adults in the school environment. When I wrote the book, *Do You Know Enough About Me to Teach Me?*, I noted the critical importance of developing significant relationships to advance the work of schools. Kordel was interested in my sports background. He heard through the "street committee" (as everyone called their source of information) that I played high school basketball and achieved a full scholarship to play at the collegiate level. That was our connection and that allowed me to begin mentoring him as a student-athlete. *He gave me permission* to inspire him (more on this later.)

Sharing my story with him without discouraging him would

present a challenge. I had the same dreams, just a different sport. I'd been preparing all my life to play professional basketball and thought I'd done all the right things and played college ball, but my name would not be called at the NBA Draft. Our conversations at lunch would soon become focused on college scouts coming to meet and visit with him, as well as the importance of keeping his grades up. Regardless of what you might read, it is important to note, all athletes aren't one dimensional. Kordel boosted a 3.5 G.P.A. His academic success was as important to him, his mother, and his family as his athletic success. As one might imagine, the young ladies at school thought highly of him. That would lead to many conversations that I hope continue to put things in perspective for him. Many of our young Black males grow up without fathers in the home. When we fail to step up in our schools to fill that gap, we fail our students. The great ones accomplish this without complaints. They understand the need outweighs the effort and they have produced evidence (successful students) over the years that continue to inspire them to give so much.

Kordel had an amazing senior year, including an opening game touchdown catch that won the game in the last seconds and was captured on film for the documentary. As his senior year progressed, Kordel would often ask questions that I had to reflect upon before answering, oftentimes saying to him, *let me think about that one*. I never wanted to lead him or any of our students down the wrong path and I think he began to appreciate the fact that I wouldn't just respond with words, but with sensible, thoughtful answers to his questions. Most notable was his appreciation of *having someone listen.* It is important to note, students pay more attention to our actions than our words.

ACTIONS VS WORDS

This would prove pivotal after football season when the applause from game-winning touchdowns couldn't be heard and those college scout visits seen on tv didn't resemble his current reality. I shared that the same thing happened to me during my senior year, but in the end, he would, as I had, be offered scholarships to play the sport he loved. In the meantime, my advice to him was to enjoy his senior year and continue to work hard in the gym and in school. Kordel is the kind of person, upon meeting him, that you walk away feeling that he is going to be successful in any field or at anything he chooses to pursue.

While dealing with the usual and unusual issues teenagers and student-athletes face, he always had his eyes on the prize. I believe his main focus though, was his mom. She was his foundation, encourager, and a consistent support system. Though there were others (his aunt), his mother symbolized why his trials would matter little in his pursuit of a better life for him and everyone in his family. His success would not be a singular feat; it was for everyone who had invested in him, a return on their investment. Ultimately, and after some disappointment, he was signed by a local university and played football for them for four years. More importantly, he graduated on time with honors and is now in graduate school in Texas pursuing his M.B.A.

There is nothing more fulfilling than seeing with your own eyes, the pursuit of excellence and the unexpected achievement that comes as a result. Successful leaders and teachers have their hearts in their purpose and their purpose in their hearts. What began six years ago continues to be a great mentor-mentee relationship. He continues his quest to be the best possible version of himself. I received a text message from Kordel today. I guess you could say that we are still sharing a word from time-to-time.

One Opportunity

As you entered Morgan County High School, the wall was decorated with student accomplishments. Now this wall was massive... one huge bulletin board from floor to ceiling and twelve feet wide. A lot of wall space at the absolute prime spot in the school. If you walked in the front door, your first few steps were alongside this wall, which became The Wall of Fame. Jennifer Butler (amazing graphic design teacher) and her students were in charge of the project. Each year, they created a new theme and design for the board, which began in August as a blank slate. By the end of the year, it was filled with pictures and captions of students who had achieved at a significant level of accomplishment. There, you would find members of the All-Region Volleyball team next to State Finalists in Extemporaneous Speaking. Art Show Medalists and Football Stars.

And, making it each week a new recipient of The Good Dog Deed Award. (Our school's mascot being the Bulldogs) Each Friday during our announcements (MCHS Live! Morgan County High School's Top Rated Televised Show: Full Disclosure- our only televised show), we presented the Good Dog Deed Award. Students and teachers nominated... other students, other teachers for having done things or been people who were "Good 'Dogs." Sometimes someone who lost their phone would nominate the person who found it and returned it. (Reunited, and it feels so good.) On other occasions, students would nominate teachers who went out of their way to help them. It was a weekly representation of the many "Good Dog Deeds" that were happening in our school community. The recipient was an example of those good deeds lifted up as such and earned a carabiner in the shape of a dogbone (woof) and coupons for ten wings or chicken tenders at Zaxby's. (woof, woof!)

We recognized the Good Dog Deed winner weekly for years and years. It was a part of our culture and it came up frequently. I'd be at the grocery store and would see one of our kids and they'd be pushing stray carts back to the store. They'd yell out, "hey, Good Dog Deed Doc! Right?!?" To which I'd always reply, "we want all of our dogs to be Good Dogs. Thank you!" (woof woof woof)

If you're not a school person you may be thinking, Wall of Fame? Good Deed Awards? That's cute, but this was a high school, did your students really get motivated with this?

Yes.

Yes, they did, and here's more. It wasn't only about motivation or inspiration. It was about opportunities. On that Wall of Fame, I wanted to recognize achievement. I wasn't trying to find something to put everybody's picture on the wall. What I did want was to create equitable opportunities for all of our kids to be successful and to be recognized if their performance warranted it. See, we were after equitable opportunities and equitable outcomes. To get to that place, you have to create conditions in which your students can think, respond, and act. Recognition of your well-earned achievement is something we all need. We believe in the recognition, but we equally believe in the well-earned achievement. And to get there, you have to be very intentional in connecting students to opportunities.

If you're a principal and people outside of school ask you "what do you do?", there are a lot of ways you can go with that. You can go for the humorous, the comprehensive, the vague, the job description... here is one you can try if you'd like. Broker of Opportunity. If you prefer, Opportunity Broker. You are uniquely positioned to know people and possibilities, and if you choose to invest the time, you can connect them together. Teachers can too, for sure. In fact, collectively we can become a school of opportunities. Those opportunities need to be offered in a manner in which we include and involve as many of our students as we can.

Which is why on the Wall of Fame, the Good Dog Deed Award Winner is displayed right next to All State Basketball. Both of those things are important. Both are accomplishments. Both matter as a part of our school community, and when we celebrate both, we are establishing our priorities. We talked about them a lot at MCHS, and shared them this way:

Do you want your classroom/school/system to address all three of these? How do you do that? An important part of this is the idea of giving everyone an opportunity to shine. And not just one, but lots of chances.

When we think about One Opportunity, the idea is this: *it might take just one thing to change the course and trajectory of a young person's life*. You know plenty of stories right now that come to your mind about someone who was given their opportunity and it made all the difference.

That's not to say that people *only* get one shot, one

opportunity (no disrespect intended to Marshall Mathers). It's the idea that *more* opportunities mean more chances to connect in a way that is *transformative*. Much of school can be very transactional, but we want to create the conditions for that which transforms the thoughts, the actions, and the possibilities for our students.

Here's a sobering note: many "one opportunity" stories were born from fate smiling on somebody and not from an intentional effort to give every one a turn at accomplishment, a turn at recognition, a turn at being a part of things. We need for schools to be havens of hope and outlets of opportunity. That's a key component of the "One" school and system. Making connections isn't only about connecting people to each other; it's also about connecting *people*... students, teachers, parents... *to opportunities*. And opportunities are just that. Not a guarantee of success, but a chance for it. When our people make their way and earn their accomplishments, we recognize them. Because... recognition is validation of *this* person while also serving as hope for the *next* one.

Nick Walker's Seizing Opportunity Every Day

It was May. The Morgan County High School tennis team was hosting the state playoffs and I was watching our team play. Out of the corner of my eye, I saw two juniors walking toward me. When you're a high school principal, you're basically like RoboCop. You have that super-speed processor going at all times, identifying situations, preparing your response. So, in an instant, I evaluated the situation: two Junior boys... it's May. One of them wants to ask a 22-year-old to the prom... going to show me a picture of her... answer... No.

All of that rolled through my processor in a nano-second, because, hey... that's what we do as principals. It was always a point of pride for me as a principal to be approachable, but I could tell these guys had something on their mind and I was sure I'd figured it out.

They came closer.

"Guys."

"Doc."

"What's happening guys?

"Nothing much. Just watching the tennis match."

My experience told me that they had completed the niceties and now we'd get down to business.

"Hey Doc..."

"Yes..." (preparing in my mind the reminder that 22-year-olds are not eligible to come to our prom)

"... um, do you know Nick Walker?"

My Robocop sensors sounding off in my head... red lights flashing in my brain... a voice saying... *alert... alert...*

"Of course, I know Nick Walker."

"Do you know that he holds the door for all of the students every day at lunch?"

"Yes... I see him do that."

"And, every day, he goes to the office and tells the ladies that work there that they're beautiful."

"Yes, Nick is a charmer, for sure. But why are we talking about him, guys?"

They looked at each other and then replied. "We want to give him a plaque."

"Oh, that's great guys. Very thoughtful. We have Award Night coming up soon and I'll put you on the agenda and you can give him his plaque there."

If you've ever worked in schools and with kids or teenagers, you know how it looks when you've given them the wrong answer. This was one of those times. "So, what is it...?"

"We don't want to give him a plaque at awards night. We want to give it to him in front of all of the students and all of the teachers."

"So, you want to have an assembly."

"Yes, that's right!"

"So, let me get this right. You two guys want to get all 1000 students and 120 staff members together so you can give one kid a plaque?"

"Yes. That's right. He's the best kid we've got."

"Well," I said, "I think this is a great idea." I went on to explain to them that we are definitely a school of 'Yes', but it's up to them to make their idea happen. "All right, we have one more time built into the schedule that we can have an assembly and it's next Wednesday. It's Thursday afternoon. If you want to make this a go, I need to see what you're going to put on the plaque by lunchtime tomorrow (Friday). I'll pay for the plaque, and let the teachers know to come to the gym next week, but you guys are in charge of the rest. Is that good?"

So, the juniors, not in search of a prom date after all, turned and walked away, talking to each other excitedly.

Honestly, I watched the tennis match, did some work, went home and never thought about it again until the next day. It's not that I don't have faith in kids, I do. It's just that when you embrace ideas, you learn that people don't always get the implementation part down and I wasn't sure about this one. No problem if they didn't-- their thought itself is kind and the sort of thing to make you proud of the kids at your school, but all ideas don't have follow-through attached.

This one did.

The next morning, they met me at the entrance of the school. Legal pad in hand. I read what they wanted inscribed on the plaque. Asked them to meet with Susan Beasley in the office to pick out what they wanted, to get in touch with Anne Stamps in the gym, and told them they had their assembly! It was Friday, and they had until Wednesday to get it all together.

If you want people to learn, you have to let them have a chance to do so. Our students always were up front at pep rallies and most assemblies, so it's not unusual for our students to take charge and learn by doing it. This was a little different since... it's these two guys putting on an assembly for one student.

On Friday, and again on Monday and Tuesday I'd see the guys occasionally in the hall and I'd say "Guys!", and they'd say "Doc!", and I'd ask them if they had it, and they said they did. They said they had it, and so, I let them run with it.

I'd let the faculty know that we had an assembly, and other than that, I didn't really do anything. Or know what the boys had planned. They said they had it and that was good enough for me. So, on Wednesday, we call the students and the teachers to come to the gym. Just as I was about to leave the office, Chad Foster, friend, local resident and educational author appeared at the office. I had wanted to connect with him, so when he said, "do you have five minutes?", I said, do you have 20 minutes? We're about to do something cool.

Chad joined me and we went to the gym, sitting in the stands. As usual, students were in charge, and my two Juniors, Jared and Tyler, grabbed a microphone and went to mid-court.

"Students, teachers, staff, we are here today to celebrate one of our best students!"

Then, from beyond the baseline, I saw two lines of football players coming into the gym. Over the gym speakers, our fight song was playing. The football players, wearing their jerseys, made a tunnel through the gym. From another part of the gym, out came the cheerleaders. If you're like me and live in the Southeast, if we have one cheerleader, we have 31 cheerleaders, and there they all were, dressed in cheerleader gear, pom poms waving and headed up into the stands.

We clearly have gone well past handing someone a plaque. It was incredible. And amazing.

The cheerleaders went into the stands and retrieved Nick Walker. At this point, if nothing else had happened, Nick Walker would still have been pretty happy.

More things happened. The cheerleaders brought Nick through the tunnel the football team had made, as those players high-fived Nick and cheered for him. All of the students were on their feet by now as Nick made it down the length of the court to the other baseline where a special chair was set up for him.

What happened next, you may not believe, but you should, because it really happened.

Those junior boys from Friday to Wednesday had planned a celebration for Nick. Students and teachers came to the microphone one after another and stood by Nick and spoke of what all he had done for them and for others. The chorus came out and sang... *You've Got a Friend in Me* from Toy Story, at which point most of the 1000 students and 120 faculty and staff members seemed to have gotten an instantaneous case of the sniffles.

Then, from the far corner of the gym, they came in. If you're a school person, you'll get this; if not, you're probably going to find it... well, never mind. From the far corner of the gym, they came in. Far from their natural habitat. There they were in our gym. The Lunch Ladies.

If you work in a school you know that those ladies (and gentlemen at many schools) work extremely hard and never have occasion to get out of the cafeteria area. But on this day, this glorious day, there they were. And our students and teachers cheered for them while they waved to the crowd. Picture the opening ceremony of the Olympics? That's what it looked like. It was awesome.

Snapping out of the wonder of this moment and coming back to matters at hand, Rhonda McCoy, our head dietitian, grabbed the microphone. With one hand leaning on Nick's special chair, and the other holding the microphone, Miss Rhonda shared these words. "Nick, everyone knows that you hold the door open every day for all of the students to come into the lunchroom. What they don't know is that every day you come into the kitchen while we're cooking, and you know all of my ladies by name, and you ask them about their family, and you tell them they look beautiful. You make this job a pleasure to come to, Nick."

And with that Miss Rhonda and her crew turned and left as quickly as they had come, once again to a standing ovation and cheers. Think of the closing ceremonies at the Olympics.

After that, there were some individual songs performed for Nick. Some more testimonials. Then the final two pieces of the day. First, Meredith Holloway, one of Nick's teachers, walked across the gym and did the most powerful thing I'd ever seen in a school.

Microphone in hand, she turned to the crowd, 1000 students and 120 faculty and staff and said, "If Nick Walker has personally done you a favor, been kind to you, please stand up."

At least 95% of the place stood. And clapped. For Nick. Who had personally done a kindness to almost everyone in the school. You know, *every one* had the same opportunity to do this, but Nick Walker... he seized the opportunity to do good. Every day.

Meredith returned the microphone to Jared and Tyler who, after a solid hour of awesomeness, were ready to give Nick his plaque. They read the inscription to all of the students and all of the teachers, just as they had asked.

To Nick Walker. Mr. Morgan County.

Thank you for teaching all of the students and teachers of our school how we should treat each other.

Chad Foster, sitting next to me, nudged me and said, "I want to start the Nick Walker Award. Every year, let's recognize the person who teaches people how to treat each other." I said, "Cool!" Then Chad said, "and the first winner is Nick Walker...", to which I replied, "Good Choice!"

So, Nick ended up at Award Night after all, becoming the first recipient of the Nick Walker Award and the only one yet to have a school-wide assembly to honor him. Throughout the next school year, Nick would come up to me in the hall, most every day and say... "Doc... I have my eye on some kids who might be good candidates for.... (dramatic pause)... The Nick Walker Award."

Part II. The Promise of Everyone.

In the first segment of this book, we explored the Power of One. We shared examples from the "individual" lens of One, showing how a focus on each and every one provides equitable opportunities and outcomes for the children and young people entrusted in our care. In this section, we draw your attention to the other side of the coin... the collective piece of One. Coming together as One. And, as challenging as it can be to provide individually for the people in your school space, that's the easy part. This is much more difficult. As a classroom teacher, you are well-versed in differentiation, RTI and MTSS so you can get your head wrapped around an individual approach to meeting your learner's needs. If you're in school leadership you know that it takes a variety of approaches and a listening ear to best serve your teachers and your staff.

"One" is a two-sided coin. As a model for classroom and school organization, One means that every person in our school world should be valued, respected, and listened to. Every one. It means that we have high expectations for our interpersonal behavior among our peers, colleagues, and those we supervise or support.

The other side of the coin is where we pick up in this section. One side of the coin stands for every one; the other stands for everyone. It means we come together as one. From different pathways, with different backgrounds; with different priorities, carrying unique exposures and experiences. We are different, but we come together as One.

This is the more difficult side of the coin. On the other side, you can, along with others, do well at doing good. You can work on your heart and your head and be a more improved version of you that sees the less-visible and notices the unnoticed. You can train your mind and establish habits and improve at serving the One.

But bringing everybody together as One? This isn't the work-based side of the coin. It's the relational side. And not just you and other people, but other people and... even more other people! This part of One isn't as easy to grasp hold of.

Here's what it boils down to:

- to reach every one, you have to believe;
- to reach EVERYONE, you have to believe SO MUCH that you can get others to believe too.

And that's the part that stops a lot of well-minded people from truly embracing the philosophy of One. Not taking anything anyway from those who can get individualized service to others right. That genuinely is great progress and will be noticeable to others. This side of One... bringing others together with each other... requires a more public posture. You can tend to individuals' needs on the other side of the coin and do so without completely immersing in the entire piece. But when you decide that you'll be a part of bringing everyone in your class/school/system together as One, you'll lose all of your anonymity. You will be behaving boldly. You'll have to explain what you mean about everyone coming together as one. You'll have to clear away enough of your doubts to be able to be convincing.

When we come together as one, it stops being about control and becomes about influence, and not everyone likes that shift. You can't make someone choose to be a part of the whole; you can't make others think outside of their own self interests. You can't make your students be nice to others when no one is looking. You can't make your teachers be a part of "all of us for all of the kids" unless they choose it. You can't make One happen.

But, you can influence others to come together. The most likely scenarios to bring people together are a common threat or a common mission. We utilize the "common threat" proviso famously in schools, with teachers and with students. Our threat is from outside... it's the governing body. Their tactic? Testing! Moreover, the way this threat plays out is not actually the testing... that's the instrument. The threat's teeth can be found in the reporting of test results, specifically in comparison to other schools, systems, or even states. And, if the report doesn't do enough on its own merits, it is often reduced to something even a passer-by will understand: a letter grade.

We actually do *come together as one* because of this threat. We have pep rallies for the test with our students (I gagged twice while typing that, sorry... need a moment), we put up huge posters about the test, and we have a competition of sorts with neighboring counties, schools, or even states. Why do we do all of these things? We've decided (or someone decided for us) that the tests are important. The coming together part? We do that to fight off the external threat.

This book isn't an anti-standardized testing book (but contact us if you'd like to talk about that ;) they have their place and that's a very long conversation. We bring it up because it's a readily-available example of how to bring people together as one. The threat of public or private shame over test scores is a powerful motivator to bring the people of the school together. Because of the near-universal nature of testing (and reporting ranked scores), nearly every school coalesces around preparation for and emphasis on the test. And before you extol the virtues of assessment, hey, we're with you. But this doesn't collect the oxygen it does if we were only assessing student progress for the purpose of improving instructional planning. Stop reporting scores outside of the school and see what happens. Behaviors would change in the absence of the threat.

Again, not here to litigate testing. Just want to use it as an example of one of the driving forces that bring people together. It's not only test reporting, but other things that are threats that unite us in purpose and action. On a much more somber note, the threat of violence brought into our schools from outside unites us in our preparations for such an event and in our hopes that we'll never have to use those protocols. Weather threats unite us in purpose and action. (see "Snowmageddon, Atlanta, 2014") On a more-limited basis, some schools have threats of closure or consolidation that bring the people there together in deep and meaningful ways.

We don't have to wait on a threat to bring people together as one. People also unite behind a cause, a mission, a purpose.

Bringing everyone together as one happens triumphantly at schools everywhere. We all have been a part of it, we've all seen it, we have been inspired by the spirit it brings. Many of these moments of triumph are born of challenge and struggle—the school coming together for a student who has lost her home; rallying together to raise money for a cause; and a classroom of kiddos shaving their heads in support for a classmate who has lost their hair during chemotherapy.

The school as its own community is built to spring into action as a group when crisis calls upon us. These times, not wished for by anyone, reveal our better natures and our capacity to set aside differences to align our resources for a common good.

If you can grab that feeling and utilize it without the instance of a crisis or a prevailing threat, what would that look like? The answer to that can lead you deeper into an exploration of how you bring lots of people together to act as one. In the following pages, we share the "how" to that question. Through examples from our time in schools, we share what we have learned works to bring every one together as one.

A Vision of Excellence for Everyone

Vision is one of the most powerful elements of any collective effort. It also seems to be among the least-understood and most-underutilized in many of our schools. Take our efforts to get students to do things in our classes and in our schools. We have ever-expansive systems that focus on response to behaviors, but very few that engage the powerhouse that is vision. Dr. Kenn Barron of James Madison University's Motivation Research Institute (MRI) makes it very clear: $M = E * V - C$. Motivation equals Expectancy times Value, minus Cost. In schools we spend some more time on the value proposition and not enough of the *expectancy* which is all about one's vision.

We have elaborate systems to increase the value proposition in the minds of our students (and teachers) of those behaviors and responses we'd like to see. I'd be comfortable in taking the side of the argument that a very-high percentage of our efforts to motivate students to do what we'd like them to do and refrain from behaviors we don't like are grounded in value, either from a positive or negative approach.

Don't believe us? Take a look at your handbook. Bet you have a section devoted to the range of consequences for certain student behaviors. I'll wager to guess that you also have a portion on grading that is deployed to shape desired academic behaviors.

Now, pull out that section on vision. On seeing possibilities and choosing behaviors that lead to those desired results.

Is your statement on vision at a meta level, for the school at large? Is it the same for everyone? Has it been the same since the last accreditation process?

Vision means much more than a vision statement for the school or system (which often are actually mission statements mislabeled as vision statements, but more on that another time). Vision is quite literally being able to see some future event. Through vision, we find efficacy, and as the MRI explains, efficacy is a pivotal part of the motivation equation. Using it as a formula, you can promise a student nearly anything under the sun, but if their vision of success is, like... zero? Do the math. $M = E * V - C$. If expectancy (E) is zero, then motivation (M) is going to equal zero. Even if value (V) is... infinite, if expectancy is zero, motivation isn't there.

Want to do equity work? Here's a *great* place to focus. Students who have the privilege of networks of support, experiences to explore, and exposure to more things often develop a greater vision, a deeper expectancy of what they can accomplish. While you're busy handing out "Eagle Bucks" to attempt to increase a student's perceived value in the behavior you're seeking, you're missing out on the *actual* difference maker in motivation. If I can see myself doing it (the task, the project, the learning) I can probably find some value on my own for doing it. If I *can't* see myself as successful... if I don't have that experience to activate at this particular time, then you don't have enough M&Ms for me to try. Because I don't want to fail; school has taught me that failing is bad.

Expectancy is being able to see the potential in doing what you haven't yet done. So, if we want our students (and our adults in the building too... consider the same in this thought process) to be motivated to do something, we ought to work on their belief that they *can* do something. And that means we need to get better at helping people see themselves as capable of completing a particular task. Our likelihood of seeing ourselves as being able to do something is benefitted when we can recall (and see again in our minds) a previous time in which we were able to accomplish something else. If you don't have a recollection of yourself as being successful, it's really hard to see a new time when you are successful.

You know how we like to take students out of things that they are good at to spend more time on things that they aren't doing well in? We think that's a grand idea, but if you do the math of the equation for motivation, it's not a very sound strategy. Students... children, adults, all of us... need to be able see ourselves being successful before we can muster up enough vulnerability to give something new a try. For students who see school as a place in which they have rarely been successful, the environment itself stymies their vision and minimizes their willingness to give tasks their maximum effort. This isn't cured by a token economy, giving 'zeros' on assignments, or "discipline" protocols. If you want someone to be successful, they need to see themselves being successful.

Vision is underutilized on the *every one* level, and we have to guard against missing its possibilities for everyone. One of the questions I like to ask students when I'm meeting with them on a school visit is this: if you could go to a different school than this one, which one would it be, and why? This question gets at the heart of what individual students think about their school: how they see it, and what possibilities they see there. Schools that are intentional in their focus on a collective vision build a culture of that vision at the school, and that vision influences the way individuals see themselves. I've been to schools that seem to be in constant struggle and in a never-ending rut. Those schools are filled with students and adults who can't see themselves doing well... can't see themselves as successful.

How do you change that? If that's not how things are at your school, how do you avoid ending up there? An ongoing examination and exploration of your core values and your vision. Individually and collectively. When done well, the two lenses (individual and collective) support each other and clarify the path ahead for every one and everyone. When you can see where you're going, it's easier to move forward and to make progress.

In this section of the book, we're focusing on the collective... the coming together. What you just read about motivation sounds a lot like it could have been in part one, the individual. Yes, the work of *One* is more connected than discrete. When you're working to build the collective strength, you begin with the growth of the individual. And... when you want to help individuals grow, you can do so more effectively via the collective. They really do connect and support each other.

Case in point, vision. One's personal expectancy, or vision can be a determinant in their success. So can the *environment* that you're in. If you go to/work at a school whose vision drives thoughts and actions in a positive way, it can have an influence on you individually. Iron sharpens iron. Game recognizes game. There's a lot of talk about *expectations* around schools and school leaders. Expectations are the byproducts of vision. If you don't invest in your vision every day, your expectations aren't pathways to promise; they're just rules and mandates.

Vision is the intersection of relationships and expectations. It's connecting people to possibilities. Helping the classroom/school create and develop a clear vision is one of the most important things a teacher/leader does.

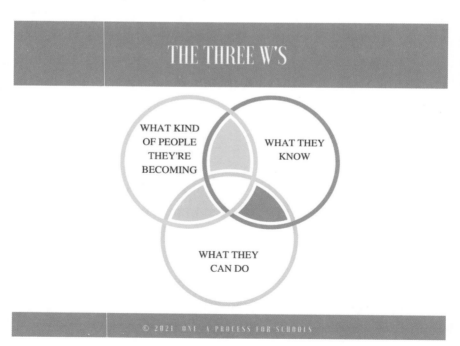

THE THREE W'S

WHAT KIND OF PEOPLE THEY'RE BECOMING

WHAT THEY KNOW

WHAT THEY CAN DO

© 2021 ONE. A PROCESS FOR SCHOOLS

A Vision to Lead, A Vision to Learn

Helping others succeed has always been my passion. There is no greater feeling in the world than coming alongside someone and empowering them to achieve their goals and vision. A few years ago, after speaking to educators around the country and reflecting on the work we do, I made a life-changing decision. I decided to get off the road and go back into a school as a high school principal.

For years, I was coaching, advising, speaking, and supporting the efforts of school leaders, teachers, and communities. So many things were changing in education and the footprints of leadership weren't the same. Social media became a dominant force and students found it increasingly more difficult to sit and listen to their teachers lecture in a classroom. The landscape of public education changed, and I found myself feeling an insurmountable pressure to deliver relevant speeches to audiences that deserved the very best I could offer.

Going back into a school building after years of being called 'an expert' had its own pressure. Having served as a middle school principal at two different schools in two different states, I was comfortable with my leadership ability and confident in my communication style of leadership. Still, the high school experience would offer challenges in a multitude of ways. Prepared to embrace these challenges, I knew the critical nature and importance of getting to know our team and the key players on our team.

At this point, you're probably thinking about positions and

titles versus people. If so, don't feel you were wrong to do so. I was referring to the students. Every teaching and leadership experience I've ever had has taught me lessons. Some have been subtle and others, more dominant. The dominant ones are like permanent tattoos; they never go away, and the lessons are there whenever we look at them. My decision to "go back to school" would change the trajectory of my thoughts, actions, and reactions. It would turn out to be one of the hardest, but best decisions I've made in my lifetime.

At this point, you're probably asking, "why?" That's a good question. The answer is, we spend our time listening to the voices of people telling us we should try this, do that, purchase this program, and go see that program. With a little research, we would probably discover, the larger percentage of those telling us these things haven't been in a classroom (teaching), or in a school (leading) in a long time. In some instances, never. The scary part of this scenario is ... we listened. I didn't want to be on that list. I believe in order to suggest something to educators, you need to be a credible source of the information you're suggesting. So, I made the decision to go back on the front lines of this work and grant access to a film crew to capture it all because I wanted educators to have an opportunity to not only hear my voice but see our work and realize our vision.

Entering the building at 6 a.m. on the first day will be a moment I'll never forget. So many students showed up hours before the first bell would ring. That was one of my first lessons. Our students were hungry; literally hungry.

Two days later, I received a call from the BBC in London. They heard about my new endeavor and had been following my education journey for years. After writing the book, *Do You Know Enough About Me to Teach Me?* and being featured on *Oprah,* my work had traction. The BBC thought it would be a good idea to send a crew to South Carolina, where the high school was located and film a documentary on the journey we were launching. An agreement was reached and approved for them to have unprecedented access to everything that happened daily, for the entire school year. Not only would we be doing important work for the community, but it would be chronicled throughout the year for other educators to see our vision in action through our work.

The work began and never stopped. As we developed and adopted the vision for Orangeburg-Wilkinson High School, (O-W) there were many doubters. I wasn't one of them. I knew the potential for O-W was there. They had championship caliber teams in football and basketball nearly every year. As a youngster growing up in South Carolina, my high school dreaded getting on the bus to travel to Orangeburg to play O-W in any sport. I was the captain of our basketball team and could never sleep the night before games against O-W. However, the expectations for academics weren't the same as they were for athletics.

Fast forward, years later: my journey, once in a school bus, now via a long career in education led me again to O-W. With our team it was time to begin our work with expectations of success. Our vision? Develop the same pride and performance academically as O-W had been known for athletically. With that vision in mind, we now had focus and purpose. I was back at O-W, this time not on the visiting team, but as the principal.

As the principal, you are measured by the quality of the team you develop. Intentionally, I've always tried to surround myself with people more talented and smarter than me. You have to train your mind to be comfortable with this in order to empower your team to function at its highest possible level. To bring about sustainable success to a classroom, school, or system, you have to be humble, focused on students, and full of passion.

Great educators are servant leaders who humbly fight for their students with a warrior spirit. At O-W, this warrior spirit already existed in the halls, gymnasiums, football fields, and hearts of our team, students, and community. Our vision and goal was clear: activating and extending that spirit to our classrooms where teaching and learning intersect.

What vision can do for a classroom, school, or system is critical. A vision is important for schools (West-Burnham, 2010) because it:

- provides the focus for all aspects of organizational life;
- informs planning and the development of policies;
- clarifies and prioritizes the work of individuals;
- helps to articulate shared beliefs and develop a common language, thereby securing alignment and effective communication;

- characterizes the organization to the rest of the world.

The vision is much more than a few words of vague intention; it embodies the values of the community and is the foundation for actions that will lead to school improvement. It brings many together as one.

Vision is only realized when leaders are able to develop and communicate it effectively with others, bringing their thoughts and talents together to create a synergy for change. Our vision at O-W positioned all of us to be successful by creating conditions necessary for success. We simplified the complexities of our work by focusing on our vision, goals, and purpose.

A vision is a picture of where you're headed. It says more than you can communicate in words. It gives others the latitude needed to see the direction. Schools are too complex to have a guide for every action that needs to be taken. That's one of the reasons that a vision is so critical. It gives the people on your team something to aim toward and that helps them know how to steer to get there. A good vision provides these things:

- Clarity: A clear picture of where we want to head. A destination that we use to model our paths after as we move towards it.

- Positivity: Acknowledge the difficulties, but don't try to motivate yourself or others with a vision of bad things that might happen if you don't succeed. Often failure is the launching pad for success. A vision rooted in fear may help fuel immediate action but can also limit your results to damage control rather than getting to positive change.

- Magnitude: Create a picture of a more distant place we're going rather than a solution to an immediate problem. A vision that's too small may not provide enough inspiration, or generate enough energy, to get you past the tough spots. It might even close your mind to what you could achieve.

- Depth: The challenges you see in front of you are only the part of the problem you can see. The rest of the challenge may be deeper and involves deeply seated beliefs that require people to challenge their own assumptions in order to move forward. Prepare for the whole journey, not just the immediate road in front of you.

You can think about this process like you're going somewhere in a vehicle. It's like this:

- **Vision** is out in the horizon, a place ahead that we think about, talk about and want to reach. It's the "there" in *Are We There Yet?*

- **Mission** is the space you can readily see out of your windshield. Keep it in the road and move forward meaningfully.

- **Purpose** is why you ever got in the car to begin with.

- **Values** are what you brought with you on this ride. You probably got some of them on previous rides. You may even pick up some new ones on this ride.

- **Strategy** is how you'll navigate the journey. Beware of potholes, and detours. There are dangers on the road too. Use your GPS to collect the data to keep you moving forward.

- **Celebrations** keep your momentum going when you're on a long ride. It's passing landmarks, crossing the border into different states, and having ice cream.

- **Wisdom?** It's knowing that someone was at the wheel before you and someone else will be there after you. (That's why you want to share the plans for the trip with the others you're with *before* you get out of the car, because after will be too late)

- **Success.** Which is more important, the journey or the destination? Maybe it's the company.

As you embark on your vision quest, reflect and refine your daily practices, and realize the full potential of your district or school, approach your journey from the heart. Don't try to think your way to a vision. Creating a vision that's exciting and compelling requires permission and freedom to dream. Use your imagination to see and feel what does not yet exist. Remember, a vision is not the same as goals and objectives; those come from the head. A true vision comes from the heart.

United By a Common Purpose and Actionable Goals

What do we hope to achieve by doing this?

Having had the pleasure to lead hundreds and hundreds of classes for administrators and thousands of individual coaching sessions, I've learned a lot about helping others in their work as leaders. What doesn't work is to tell them what they ought to be doing. You only learn to solve the equations by trying the equations yourself and learning to solve by first failing to solve. A good coach/teacher has to have a lot of patience and learn to avoid thinking for the student/coachee, and instead teach the student/coachee strategies in decision-making and problem-solving.

What do we hope to achieve by doing this? This question has been helpful for new and veteran leaders in matters of logistics and in hiring new staff; in student policies and in curriculum strategies. What do we hope to achieve by doing this?

In answering that question, you have to reveal your agenda. State your purpose. When we begin with what we're hoping to accomplish, it helps us develop the right strategies in how we can get it done. Often, the emerging leader realizes that what she is thinking about doing doesn't really square with her actual goal of doing so. When we crystallize our intent, clarify our purpose, and make it the top line of our agenda and the measure of our efforts, we begin to lead with the sort of direction that brings a sense of clarity to our work.

School people frequently and famously are given flashy new

initiatives, programs and ideas to implement in their buildings and classrooms. The 'what' and the 'how' of those things are often explained in detail, but in the absence of their 'why', those initiatives often fall flat. They may or may not have been good ideas, relevant and appropriate for the context in which they're introduced. Without clarity of purpose, people in schools typically assign minimal energy and engagement into something new. This is true of all of the citizens of the school: students, teachers, and staff members alike.

Simon Sinek's *Start With Why* is required reading for school leaders and a meaningful lens to examine implementation efforts for anyone. Finding relevance in the tasks we're asked to/required to do changes our approach to the work; beginning that same work with clarity of purpose is even more impactful. When we know why we're doing something, we're more likely to invest discretionary time and energy in its pursuit. When we believe in the 'why', our investment goes even deeper. And how do we deeply believe in the purpose of a thing we're doing at school? We talk about it. A lot. We make the process of *identifying purpose* universal among everyone in our organization and consistent in all affairs.

That student who asks, 'why are we doing this?' shouldn't be considered an annoyance. In turn, the teacher shouldn't expect that she has to deliver a Google-worthy answer either. That question, raised sincerely, should trigger an exploration of the overall goals of the school. Not just to be answered in some sort of defense by the teacher, but as a part of the ever-clarifying process of discovering 'why.'

Administrators can create conditions that either lead to the exploration of purpose or build a fortress of compliance by shutting down questions. One of the things some administrators say that makes me bristle the most (there *are* a few...) is this one: don't bring me a problem without bringing a solution with it. I'm sure that was borne from a place where the intention was to develop a positive work environment (see the next chapter, please) but what it really says is... keep your opinions to yourself. When that's followed by the same administrator saying to his teachers 'you really need to build relationships with your students...' the teachers are right to raise an eyebrow.

The best of organizations are constantly self-examining their actions and their intentions and reconciling the two. That's why I encourage everyone to avoid laminating your mission, vision and belief statements. What you truly believe, what possibilities and direction you see, and what actions you are currently taking can be seen in your classrooms and hallways. Some mission statements are wishin' statements; want to write an accurate mission, vision and purpose for your school or system? Get a knowledgeable, objective visitor or visitors to come to your schools, system, and classrooms. Talk to the students. Talk to the teachers. Ask them, what is it you all are trying to accomplish here? What's your purpose here? Why are you doing what you're doing right now?

You can say most anything is your mission. What counts is what you actually do.

When you get your purpose aligned, your people can walk into the school every day with confidence knowing what they're a part of. So many schools have been maligned with efforts to micromanage the work of teachers that those teachers often feel an absence of purpose, replaced with stringent guidelines of what they are to teach, when they're to teach it, and often these days, how to teach it. And when you answer all of those questions for your teachers, they may or may not even want to know why. Daniel Pink says in his book *Drive* that people are motivated by three things: Autonomy, Mastery, and Purpose. If that's true of your teachers, how do you feed them in those three areas? If it's also true of your students, when do we talk to them about these three?

And, collectively, what's our purpose as a school? As a classroom? As a school system? Does it change over time? When and how should we examine purpose?

Twenty-five thousand Handwritten Letters. In One Day.

Karl Scott came into my office full of excitement. "Hey, you've got to watch this movie."

From that simple exchange came an unlikely encounter of 1000 students, 120 faculty and staff, and a powerful exploration of purpose.

Karl taught Biology at MCHS and had previously worked in nearby Athens-Clarke County. The movie he recommended was Athens-based, featuring the story of Darius Weems, a band of friends known as his crew, and a modern-day Odyssey.

The movie, *Darius Goes West* is the story of 15-year-old Darius Weems who, like his deceased older brother, has Duchenne Muscular Dystrophy. Darius, who had rarely been out of his hometown of Athens at the time, wanted to get on MTV's "Pimp My Ride" show and get a deluxe treatment for his wheelchair. A team of friends who had promised Darius' brother that they would keep an eye on him in his absence did more than that.

They chronicled the trip from Athens, GA across the country in documentary style, traveling together in an accessible-RV on a trip funded by selling "end-credits" in advance. Crowdsourcing, early days.

The movie is an amazing story of brotherhood, of accessibility, of friendship... and Karl Scott didn't only want me to watch it, he wanted everyone to watch it. I did, and then we did. Our English teachers offered to show the movie in their classes, so between Thanksgiving and Christmas, we watched it together, as a school. Then something really incredible happened: Karl got in touch with Logan Smalley, the leader of the group, and arranged for Darius and the crew to come to MCHS.

We told the students that we were going to have an assembly on Christmas tree safety. They knew better, but they liked that they did. They had figured out that we were going to be visited by Darius and some of them even made signs to welcome him. Again, every student in the school watched this powerful movie, about a teenager like them, from a community close to us. The power of doing things together... reading a book, watching a movie, can't be overestimated. That unity gave us a unique opportunity to find purpose.

When Darius came into the gym, you would have thought that it was _____ (name your favorite movie star) or _____ (name your favorite band/group/singer). It was that level. Our kids had seen Darius take his first dip into the ocean. They'd seen him visit New Orleans, and fly in a hot air balloon. They'd seen the joys and sorrows of his life and this incredible cross-country journey. They'd seen him eat wasabi sauce, which he referred to as 'Goslabi', a name that fit and became a rallying cry for the movie and for Darius.

Our students knew all about him, and there he was, in person in our gym. Darius and the crew spoke to our students, answered questions, and then posed for pictures for a long time afterwards. It was a great day at school.

The movie's purpose (beyond the cross-country trip) was to

raise awareness and funds for DMD research. When Darius came to Morgan County, our students loved meeting him, but they wanted to do more. They had learned enough about Darius and had a personal connection in meeting him that they were driven to action. Our students had knowledge, enthusiasm, and a purpose. One after another, kids came to me that day saying those magical words, *"I want to do something."*

Nothing is sweeter to the principal's ears than a student saying *"I want to do something,"* When dozens and dozens say they want to do something? Let's Go!!! I reported to the student government leaders that their people wanted to do something. And, boy, did they.

During the announcements the following morning, students who *wanted to do something* were encouraged to come to Room 218 during the activity period that afternoon. Room 218 could hold about 40 people. It wasn't enough.

Over 200 students came that day, and the meeting was moved to the cafeteria. There, our student government folks handed out pens and paper, appointed table leaders and got a 200-person conversation going. We actually came out of that brainstorming session with several things that we did, but there was one that got everyone across the school involved.

From Karl Scott to the English teachers, from the assembly to the brainstorming, in a matter of weeks our school was preparing for this: to help raise awareness and funds for DMD research, and to help Darius, the students of Morgan County High School decided to send a copy of the DVD to every high school in America. With a handwritten letter from one of our students to recommend watching the movie. All in one day.

Funders came along to pay for the DVDs and the postage. The rest was up to our students. 25,000 high schools, 1000 students, so 25 handwritten letters in one day. Plus, stuffing all of the packages.

Guess what? They did it. It was highly-organized, of course supported by faculty. We had live music throughout the day to raise spirits and create atmosphere. Our student leaders wrote letters in advance so they could spend the day encouraging others in their work. We learned a lot of things that day:

- Nobody writes anymore. It took an incredibly long time to handwrite letters, and it took us all day to write, stuff, and prepare to mail all 25,000 items. Lots of sore hands the next day.

- Students are often underutilized in schools. The adults helped them, but our kids did this. What can the kids in your class, your school do?

- Some of our students weren't sure that we'd pull this off. After we did, it gave them a boost of confidence— individually and collectively. Nothing quite like biting off a challenge and seeing it through. Especially when you do it together.

- Purpose is contagious. Students are wired to do things together and are interested beyond themselves. When we give them the opportunity, they can rise to the expectations.

- For the record, this was a school-wide, all-day activity. It was worth every minute spent and was an opportunity for our students to learn in ways that resonated with them.

- In case you were wondering, students were writing all over the school. Having watched the movie together, met Darius and the crew in person, and then created this activity themselves, our students had a unique experience of doing things together, which was purpose inside of purpose.

This book is about you—you and your classroom, your school, your school system. It's intended to help you see that a focus on the individual and the whole are complementary and when you work to do both, you see how each supports the other. Remember when we talked about motivation? $M = E * V - C$. Expectancy. When you are successful as part of a group doing things that seemed difficult (or maybe seemed impossible), you begin to change your way of thinking about what you can *personally* accomplish. When your expectancy rises, so does your overall motivation.

Coming together as one... with a purpose ... to do something for someone else is as powerful as anything you can do to "raise student achievement." Want to know how our academic performance rose every single year? And how we were named a National Model School four times? While others were sending their students to double and triple math segments, we were focused on who our students were becoming as people. How they viewed themselves. How they interacted with each other and the world. We focused on creating conditions for them to have unique learning experiences. We emphasized the beauty of the struggle that leads to success. People with purpose see possibilities, promise, and potential. People without it see compliance, and annoyances, and school being done *to* them. Which paradigm do *you* choose?

A Prevailing Attitude That Makes Everyone Better

Ever been somewhere that everyone who worked there was... really nice? That the people there tried to make things easier for you? Where it seemed that you were valued and that the people who were working there enjoyed it?

Now. Ever been somewhere that's just the opposite? Where it seems like everyone's unhappy? They have a sign in the front office that says this: I can only solve one problem a day. Today's not your day. Tomorrow's not looking good either.

I have. I've been to both of those places, actually more than once... multiple locations. And, they were all schools.

I've been to schools where I smiled when I pulled into the parking lot because I had been there before and remembered what it was like. Not just about what they said to me or how quickly they answered the door. No, these schools make me happy to get there because the people inside of them are consistently positive. They are cordial to each other. The students look happy. The teachers speak to each other as they pass in the halls. And, the principal is in the smack-dab front of the lobby to greet every student... by name... and connect with them.

I've also been to schools that were... different than that. Once, I visited a school and in the main office there was a desk for one of the members of the clerical staff. On my first visit to the principal there, I noticed strips of tape on the floor near that desk in the shape of a perfect square, about a foot on each side. The tape-square was located about four feet from the clerk's desk. I went back to a conference room to wait on the principal, and it was some time before he arrived. He said he'd had to deal with some discipline cases, and was sorry to be late. We talked for a while about the school, the students, what challenges he had, and before I left I remembered to ask him what that taped-off area was for.

Come here and I'll show you, he said. We went out and there it was. A student had approached the desk while we watched and neatly lined herself up in the square. Her little sixth-grade feet fit neatly in the middle of the square, and she reached as far as she could toward the clerk's desk without her feet leaving the square. The clerk, without looking up at her, said, "okay, you can drop it now," and the student dropped off whatever paperwork she had been asked to bring to the office, and then with a quarter-turn angled herself away from the desk and back toward the office entrance.

"How about that?", the principal said. "Yes, how about that," I replied.

On my next visit there, the principal was later to meet than the first time, again, noting discipline issues. It was on that trip I asked him about "the square." He said it was there when he got there, that the secretary didn't like people leaning on her desk, and that the kids all knew to get in that square. I asked him what he thought about it, and he didn't really have much to say.

See, here's the thing. If you have constant behavioral issues with your students, it may be worth asking how the students feel about coming to school. The square in the front office was evidence of how they were looked upon by the people who work in the office, who are seen as appendages of the principal. Do your students feel like you care about them and want to protect them, or do they feel like you're afraid of them and want to control them?

Good news: we can choose our attitude. Every day, all day long. We literally *can* control this one. We spend a lot of time trying to control things that we can't (other people, how others act, the future, etc...) and not as much time as we ought to on the things that we *can* control, specifically here, our attitude and our attitude toward other people.

An attitude refers to a set of emotions, beliefs, and behaviors toward a particular object, person, thing, or event. Attitudes are often the result of experience or upbringing, and they can have a powerful influence over behavior. Researchers define attitudes as a learned tendency to evaluate things in a certain way. This can include evaluations of people, issues, objects, or events. Such evaluations are often positive or negative, but they can also be uncertain at times.

People tend to behave based on their exposure and experience, and relative to the environment they're presented. It's easier to be positive if you're around positive people. If you are around people who are consistently negative, you run the risk of falling in with them. My observation to the administrators with whom I work has always been this: the greatest influences

we can control

Choose our attitude ↓

on a teacher are the teachers in the rooms to her left, to her right, and across the hall.

That's why it's critical to coalesce around a set of attitudes that make your school a great place for students to attend AND a great place for your adults to work. There's an overwhelming tendency for behavior to gravitate to the mean. Normal distribution seems to be exactly as advertised... it's how things typically sort themselves out. About 68% of your people (students in a class or teachers in the school) will likely gravitate towards a norm for behavior, for attitudes. What's the norm at your school for how your adults think about the students? I mean, *really* think about the students? What's your faculty and staff's attitude about each other? Sometimes faculty or staff members can have conflicting feelings about a particular person or issue. It's easy to call out someone on the evaluation for a technical part of the job they haven't done well in; it's much more difficult to address *attitude*. If it's over-the-top that's one thing, but *the micro behaviors of the people of your school are the key to your success or your struggles,* and they are almost exclusively a function of attitude, which you and your team have a choice in every day.

Over time, we have come to understand that there are several different components that make up attitudes. Often referred to as the ABC's of attitude, the components listed below influence how and why attitudes are formed.

Components of Attitude

- Affective Component: How the object, person, issue,

or event makes you feel;

- Behavior Component: How your attitude influences your behavior;
- Cognitive Component: Your thoughts and beliefs about the subject.

How do schools gravitate toward either a) productive and positive attitudes or b) damaging and negative attitudes?

Well, it may have to do with the emphasis and expectations at a school-wide (or class-wide) level. Attitudes in an organization emanate from that organization's values. Sometimes the stated values of the organization are carried out in the actions of the faculty and staff and sometimes, they are not.

Making your school or classroom the place people want to be begins with a process of identifying your values as a group. Then, you examine how your actions line up with those values every day from then on. You make strides when you simultaneously talk about those values in many ways, frequently, and intentionally. In other words, your climate as a function of your culture can be left to chance, or it can be meaningfully developed. The "One Attitude" that makes the difference in the schools described above is rarely coincidental. It's positive when it gets attention; it's not when it doesn't.

There are a number of factors that can influence how and why attitudes form. Experience, social factors, learning, conditioning, and observation to name a few. In a school setting, we understand the fact that a negative attitude is ten times more powerful than a positive one. Therefore, if you have ten people on your team with positive attitudes, and one person with a negative attitude, what just happened to your team's energy? As a principal, I often reminded myself of two general rules of attitude.

1. You can't change another person's attitude, mindset, or way of thinking. You can only provide the environment for that change to occur and create the conditions.

2. The closer the person is to us, or the more value they bring, the more we have a tendency to ignore rule # 1.

Flip Flippen in his "Capturing Kids Hearts" work focuses on developing a social contract among the people in the classroom and/or school. In building that contract, the participants respond to these four questions:

1. How do you want to be treated by me? (the leader, the teacher)

2. How do you want to be treated by each other?

3. How do you think I (the leader, the teacher) want to be treated by you?

4. How do you want to treat each other when there is conflict?

In this process or processes like it, classrooms and schools become more effective through the development of an agreement on how everyone will treat each other. Like any good effort, the social contract in CKH is of little value if developed, laminated, and forgotten. Any effort to build group norms takes consistency and regular attention. The positive in that? Anyone can do it if they are willing to do it. The power of collective attitudes in a school is one of the greatest resources available and within everyone's reach.

A final note... don't expect everyone to have a positive attitude if you as the leader choose not to have on yourself. Like most everything we do in working with others, our work with *them* begins with our work on *us*. I consider myself to be a *work-in-progress*.

Not at the beginning, but not finished learning and growing. Pragmatically, the leader should *want* to activate the power of positive attitudes, and to do so understand that it has to begin... with a look in the mirror.

McKenzie

One of ten white students in a high school of eleven hundred students, McKenzie entered the scene the same time I did. We were the "newbies" at "O-W" and our orientation period didn't last long. As principal, I found myself watching out for her without knowing the specificity of what I might be looking for. Having been in a situation like this before in another state and school, I realized we develop the mental capacity to draw inference from past experiences. Our past experiences grant access to patterns, behaviors, and outcomes. I would need every resource available to help provide what we see in almost every mission statement in schools, "a safe and orderly environment for teaching and learning."

McKenzie didn't take long making friends with other students and didn't appear to be uncomfortable in her new school setting. The cafeteria is a place where stories are told and unfold so I paid close attention to conversations and watched body language throughout the three lunch periods scheduled throughout the day. On the third day of McKenzie's new experience, I was called to a classroom where an altercation was taking place. In the middle of the action was none other than our new student, McKenzie. After separating what was considered to be a pretty ugly fight, I was able to have McKenzie escorted to my office. She was very upset and crying, struggling to catch her breath. After a few moments and between deep pauses, she was able to explain to me what happened in room 204.

One of her new friends was engaged in a conversation about a boy with another female classmate. The conversation started getting loud and before the teacher could get between the two students, a fight broke out. As the teacher stepped in between the two students, McKenzie, who couldn't believe what she was seeing, told one of the girls that she was wrong to start fighting over a boy with her newfound friend. Lesson number one; never step into a situation that has nothing to do with you, especially at "O-W". A second fight began, this one between another girl and McKenzie. As McKenzie explained to me, "it was her or me" and my mouth dropped open. Over the years, I have seen many things in the schools I've served, but never what I was witnessing on that day. After a box of tissues and two bottles of water, McKenzie and I were ready for some "real-talk."

We were also ready to ask McKenzie's mom to join us. Her mom was a manager of one of the local restaurants in our area and also, very involved in her daughter's life and schooling. I was fortunate to have an active parent who also became a school-business partner. As I prepared to explain the events of the day, she walked into my office with a worried look on her face and trauma in her eyes. You can only imagine my attempt to find the right words to say. Abandoning the coursework on school leadership and all that I've read over the years, I relied on good "old fashion" faith and truth. I looked her mother in the eyes and said, here's what happened today. The response from McKenzie's mother would facilitate a series of events that could never be scripted or planned. It was the beginning of a master lesson on life from many perspectives, a road less traveled.

McKenzie's mom was more than understanding (more than I would've been) under the circumstances. Her bottom line was, "stay in your lane, stop placing yourself in this position, and focus on your schoolwork." In classic McKenzie fashion, her neck rolled to the left, and she said to her mom and her principal, "this is the reality of school today." We were taught a lesson on how much things have changed since we were in school and how important it was for her to take a stand for her friend in their classroom. Regardless of the outcome of the physical altercation in room 204, McKenzie felt she stood up for what was right, that all students should be respectful of themselves and others. Her experience in room 204, though extremely negative, was the beginning of something special for McKenzie and many others, including me.

As one might imagine, the talk of a white female student getting into a fight with a black student at a predominately black school led the news cycle at O-W. The rest of the week would prove to many of us that we had within us the desire to confront what was staring us all in the face. Schools are a microcosm of society; we were clearly being challenged to do something to turn negative into positive. We have all heard "when we know better, we should do better." The desire we had collectively outweighed the fear many of us considered while thinking, discussing, and brainstorming ways to approach "the elephant in the room."

McKenzie resumed her class schedule after the altercation with her sights set on better and brighter days ahead. As her principal, I shared my open-door policy with her and told her I was there for all students and for some unknown reason, I knew she believed me and believed in me. Her mom called later that day and wanted to schedule an appointment to see me. As I reflected on our meeting with McKenzie and all that transpired, I wondered what might come next.

Meeting with McKenzie's mom again was always pleasant, but when a parent's child experiences a physical altercation at school, pleasantries fade quickly. Our meeting began with McKenzie's mom sharing her thoughts on my desire to make a difference in the lives of our students. Further, she stated, she could see in my eyes that it was more than a job; "more of a calling placed over my life." Tears began to form in the vessels of both of my eyes because I've always known that deep place, but didn't know how many others ventured there. She wanted to help and in doing so, proposed an idea to address an issue we talk about, but rarely do anything constructively to offset it; race.

On the other side of the city, there was another high school that starts with an O. We were O-W and they were "O-P." O-P was an abbreviation for Orangeburg Prep, a private school that was 95% white. McKenzie's mom thought it would be a great idea to propose to the principal at O-P, an exchange day. A select number of our students would do an exchange with the same number of students from O-P. That exchange would mean going to classes, eating lunch, interacting with other students, teachers, faculty, and staff. I thought it was an excellent idea and didn't hesitate to call the principal at O-P. As one might imagine, he was quiet at first, then told me he would need approval from his school board for an exchange of this nature. There was much to consider and much at stake.

After weeks of waiting, I decided to follow-up with him and even though he thought it was a good idea and could possibly serve as a springboard for discussion among students, his board was less than interested due to so many unknowns. Complicating matters further, this exchange would also be captured on film as the documentary was still being filmed during this time span.

After several calls, discussions, and careful considerations, we decided to modify our plans. We would bring several students to their school (field trip) and begin with a smaller dialogue around the subject of race. I facilitated the morning and was honored to do so. Though it wasn't the full exchange day McKenzie's mom envisioned, it was a start. She was gracious and kind enough to cater breakfast for the event and proud to be able to turn a negative into a positive.

The morning was full of promise as students from both schools engaged in conversation about their own experiences around race. Quickly, the adults in the room pondered if this is a new generation with a new generation of thought? McKenzie's enrollment in O-W opened the door to many possibilities. More importantly, it opened the hearts and minds of so many that had been closed to the unknown. Through McKenzie, we all received an education not found in textbooks, but birthed in human kindness and renewed effort; a desire we should all possess to make our schools and world a better place.

Space for Everyone's Ideas

What unites people? A good idea.

So, here's a question for you about your classroom and/or school. Are you a school of yes, or are you a school of no?

Shouldn't schools and classrooms be pools of ideas? Some are. Some aren't.

In some schools, it's easy to get to 'yes.' In others, it's so unlikely that people keep their ideas to themselves.

Back to the idea of 'One Attitude' from the last chapter, if our most deeply seated values include the way we treat others, shouldn't we have a high regard for the way we treat each other's ideas as well?

Here's a sad truth. There are people—students and adults—in every school, everywhere with great ideas. Not all of them are in an environment friendly to ideas. That gets to the nature of school at its foundational levels. We should be places of experimentation and of curiosity. I know why it's hard to do these things... *the expectation of perfection smothers the promise of progress.* When we are expected for every single thing we do within the classroom and school to be perfect in every way, we discourage the space for the untried, the original, the innovative. Those things? Yes, those are the things our students need to develop to prepare them for what lies ahead.

Please know that this isn't some admonition to you or your classroom or school, but instead an encouragement that the best learning activities in your school may be in the minds of people who don't feel confident in sharing them. I understand that you are limited by the range in which your supervisors permit you to explore. Maybe that's the central office, the school board, or your community, but within the realm you've been permitted, please encourage ideas, innovation, dreams, and experimentation.

Want to get students to work at their best? Connect their learning with their interests. Combine their dream with the curriculum. Mash up their ideas with their learning standards.

This isn't just about an idea or two that comes along everyone once in a while. If you intentionally create space in your classroom, school, or system for ideas to live, you'll have built a climate that gets your people out of bed in the morning. I've worked at both kinds of schools—the kind where the people are so paralyzed by the fear of something-might-go-wrong that they don't want to do anything. I've also worked at the kind of school where responsible freedoms permit the citizens of the school the space to create, to experiment, and to learn. If you get to that place in your classroom or school, you'll be flipping a switch that changes *everything*. It's actually pretty simple: if you're offering a dynamic environment where learning is encouraged and experiences are valued, you're going to have students and teachers who want to be there. When people *want* to do things, there's a noticeable difference in how they do them.

One person's idea can ignite another's. One student's

achievement can inspire more. An innovation can lead to a spark for another innovation. Your school is full of ideas. What would it look like if you created a space in which they were free to move about?

So much of this connects back to the notion of the One Attitude. Schools where things are 'yes' in one room and 'no' or 'NO!' in others don't blend well. It takes a positive overall school attitude about innovation and ideas to create an environment that fosters them. Once people know their innovations and ideas are welcomed, they will bring them to you.

Cicely Lewis

This is a story about Cicely Lewis, but it's also a story about Tommy Welch.

Cicely Lewis is the Media Specialist at Meadowcreek High School in Gwinnett County, GA. She was named the 2020 National School Librarian of the Year, presented by the *School Library Journal* (SLJ).

In 2017, Cicely was rolling out the theme for her library for the year. As she was decorating for the year (Harry Potter theme), she stopped to read from a copy of *Essence,* which featured a "Stay Woke" edition. She contemplated the needs of her students at Meadowcreek (2,600 Students, 70+% Latinx), the context of the moment (the Dreamer Act had just been repealed) and wanted to make reading more relevant for the students in her school.

She did not, as she has said many times since, know what all was about to happen.

Cicely introduced to her students "Read Woke" and extended the Read Woke Challenge. According to Cicely, when asked what Read Woke is:

> It's a feeling. A form of education. A call to action, and our right as lifelong learners. It means arming yourself with knowledge to better protect your rights. Learning about others so you treat people with respect and dignity, no matter their religion, race, creed, or color.

Along with support from faculty members, students began to read books about characters that look like them and represent their frame of reference. Cicely identified books for her list, developed a prize list for readers, and solicited the help of faculty to include books from the list for their reading.

The payoff? Students started reading. And they enjoyed reading.

And they weren't the only ones.

Read Woke took off. The Meadowcreek HS Printing Lab developed the iconic t-shirts. Other schools wanted to join, and Cicely developed a format and registration. What's happened is that at *hundreds of schools* students are (many for the first time) reading about characters that make them feel seen and heard.

New authors from underrepresented groups have found willing readers and are writing new books. Cicely spreads the word in a regular column for *School Library Journal.*

And then, Read Woke went international. There's Read Woke Canada, and it just landed in Scotland. It's led by Meadowcreek students who have now moved from consumers of books to *influencers* for others around the world.

So you'll know, Read Woke is an incredibly successful effort, but it's not all that Cicely Lewis, Superstar Librarian does. She delivers books to local laundromats so kids who are there have something to read. She also hosts a Prom Book Fashion Show, Library Science, and installed FitDesk Bikes so students can exercise both body and mind at the same time.

This is a story about Cicely Lewis, but it's also a story about Tommy Welch.

Tommy Welch was the principal at Meadowcreek High School where he was named the 2017 Georgia Principal of the Year (Georgia Association of Secondary School Principals) and was a finalist for National Principal of the Year (National Association of Secondary School Principals). While he served as Cicely's principal, he created an environment and culture of 'yes' to ideas.

Cicely's idea (Read Woke) has inspired literally thousands to read and encouraged thousands of educators to consider their students when selecting or offering book choices. This is a tremendously successful venture and one that is doing important work in giving voice to the voiceless and the value of reading to many who hadn't found themselves in books. Yes, this is *definitely* a story about Cicely Lewis and the power of an idea.

It's also a reminder that we have *other* good ideas that are going unspoken in classrooms and schools everywhere. What if Cicely was in a different school? Would she have been able to do what she's been able to do? (Note: Cicely *is* an amazing spirit and probably would have found a way, somehow... but it was a much more direct route in a fertile location for ideas.)

Why can't all of our classrooms be hubs of innovation? Why can't all of our schools offer faculty members a place to experiment and to provide students an experience? That's what makes school a place where people want to be. Create a place for ideas... in your classroom, in your school, in your system. You'll find that amazing ideas are everywhere, they just need the right conditions in which to blossom.

A Welcoming Place for Everyone's Voice

Students have the greatest stake in their education but little to no say in how it is delivered (Brenner,2019.) Brenner goes on to say, "this lack of agency represents a lost opportunity to accelerate learning and prepare students for a world in which taking initiative and learning new skills are increasingly critical to success." In education, student voice refers to the values, opinions, beliefs, perspectives, and cultural backgrounds of individual students and groups of students in a school, and to instructional approaches and techniques that are based on student choices, interests, passions, and ambitions.

As a school, the concept of student voice has grown increasingly popular in recent decades. Moreover, student voice can be seen as an alternative to more traditional forms of governance or instruction in which school administrators and teachers may make unilateral decisions with little or no input from students. Historically, student council and other forms of student-led government were the most common channels for students to share their opinions and viewpoints, but many of these opportunities did not allow students to make authentic contributions to the leadership of a school.

Teacher voice refers to the values, opinions, beliefs, perspectives, expertise, and cultural backgrounds of the teachers working in a school which extends to teacher unions, professional organizations, and other entities that advocate for teachers.

Leigh Colburn, national guru in student voice and the author of *The Wraparound Guide* (IPPY's Gold Medal Winner for the top Educational Resource Workbook of 2021) built a model of service to students at Marietta High School that became the template for serving students holistically through her wraparound approach. At the core of her work though, is student voice. Leigh and her team brought two powerful questions to students that would light the path to their success:

- What do you need?
- What is getting in the way of your learning?

Those questions are the openers, but it's just the starting point for Leigh, and her business partner Linda Beggs in their work as the Centergy Project. Leigh is a master questioner and gets to the core of student's needs (and subsequently a path to student success) through ongoing and in depth conversations with students. At their website, Leigh and Linda keep the conversation going, offering a place for students to "tell their story." There, anyone can answer these questions that help give an understanding to their needs:

- What was your greatest barrier to learning and graduation?
- When times were challenging, who or what gave you hope and kept you engaged?
- If you had a particular teacher who was important to you, how did he or she influence you?
- If you chose to leave high school prior to graduation, when did it begin to go off track for you? Was there something that could have been done by the school to

keep you engaged and on the path of graduating?

- Was there something important for your school to have known about you—something that would have helped school staff in teaching and supporting you—but your school never knew it?

- Do you have a significant or favorite school memory? If so, please tell us about it.

- Do you have a suggestion for improving the student experience or the way educators support students in school?

- Is there something you considered to be your greatest achievement in school?

- Where are you now? Is there something you would want to tell your school self or your school's staff?

- Is there anything else you would like to share?

What would you find about your students if you asked them these questions? Would you be able to better plan your work to connect with their needs? We often talk about *meeting students where they are.* Do you and your team need to get more specific and more intentional in what you do?

It begins by setting time for intentional conversations. Good questions. Listening. Hearing our students and what they view as a path to their needs, their passions, and their success.

Friday Alive!

"We ought to do this every week," Phillip Godwin said. It was August, during one of our lunch shifts and the commons area in front of the auditorium and cafeteria were bustling. We were holding our Club Fair during all of our lunch shifts, outside on a beautiful Friday. Dozens and dozens of clubs were represented with tables and displays, free giveaways and farm animals (different booths). In the past, this event was held indoors, during class time and instead our students had presented the idea to have it outside with a more-festive atmosphere.

Our students were absolutely having a great time. Clubs had members recruiting new members; students listened to the music we had on hand and got a shaved-ice from the stand. It was definitely a five-star day, and Phillip was onto something.

"We could have music, have bands, we can sell food, we don't have to have all of the booths, but we could have this every week," Phillip told me as we walked around the booths together. From that idea, Friday Alive was born.

On the steps of the auditorium, which made for a perfect make-shift stage, we began a tradition of celebration (most) every week, on Fridays. Phillip had a great idea; let's provide a space for our students to perform, for other students to hear them, for us to create a positive atmosphere celebrating life, school, and the accomplishment of another week of school. Over time, a set-up/stage crew became a fixture, and our student organizers began to "book" acts to play Friday Alive.

We had slam poetry and rap battles; the percussion line and the step team; bands and solo artists. Friday Alive gave a place for our students to perform and for their peers to enjoy them.

We brought bleachers over from the tennis courts across the street and set up a place for our students to grab their lunch, sit outside, and take in the show. Student groups signed up to be able to have bake sales and, most of the year (it's usually hot in Georgia), we'd also have a shave-ice booth.

Students need an outlet; they need a stage and an audience. Some of our greatest moments at MCHS happened during Friday Alive. We had the occasional karaoke episode of Friday Alive, but we also featured some amazing soloists, duos, and bands who prepared for their time on the Friday Alive stage. One of our Friday Alive performers even made it to the Grand Ole' Opry stage.

Some of the most memorable Friday Alive sets were those when our student-artists made their debut. One Friday, a freshman stood alone on the auditorium steps, guitar in place, face near the microphone, but nothing coming out. Standing nearby, I asked Ty Manning and Steve DeLaigle, teachers and musicians themselves, what was happening. Ty said, "I think he's frozen." Steve said, "Yes, he looks like he's not moving." Ty went up to him, whispered something, and then, the voice that came out? Sounded like American Idol. The Voice. It was phenomenal. Only a few years later that student was singing at Phillips Arena in Atlanta.

We learn from experiences, and school should be a place that opens the door to experiences and opportunities. At Friday Alive, our students had a chance to do what they loved in front of their peers, who learned to appreciate their courage, their performances, and their willingness to share. When students learn to cheer for each other, they begin to appreciate each other, value each other, and respect each other.

When we make school a place of experiences and opportunities, we open the door for the passions of our students. We find out, as Leigh Colburn and Linda Beggs show, their greatest needs, and we discover the things they most want to make their school experience a rich and valuable one, one worthy of a song.

A Commitment to Each Other's Well-Being and Success

In the discussion of the difference between involvement and commitment, one needs look no further than the bacon, egg, and cheese biscuit for clarity. For, in the bacon, egg, and cheese biscuit, the hen and the cow were involved; the pig, however, was committed.

You are most likely reading this book to spur your thoughts about having a more-effective classroom, school, or school system. So far, we've explored individual and collective energies that make for that kind of class or school.

This chapter is devoted to an element that is a difference-maker. It's the difference between being involved and being committed. Between being the hen and being the pig. Participating versus going all in. This chapter is about commitment. It's about gaining the commitment of the group, that inspires the commitment of the individual, that strengthens the commitment of the group.

So, here goes. There is a great deal of variance between schools. That doesn't surprise you if you're a part of the education world. In every school there are elements of good practices. There are good teachers. There are opportunities, and there are good outcomes for some students. That's probably the key: when we examine the question of "how's school?", the answer depends upon who we're asking.

That's why Stephen and I are writing this book and supporting school systems through our One. Process. Getting school right is very challenging, but it's critical. It's critical for every school. It's critical for every student in your school. And it's hard.

Everyone is working hard. I imagine Yogi Berra would say, of our current status in education, even the people who aren't working hard, they're working hard too. No one on our team questions the individual commitment of educators. No one on our team questions the hard work our teachers and school leaders are doing.

What we ask you to question, however, is this: in spite of our good intentions and hard work, are we designed for the success we are seeking?

Here are some thoughts to consider as you ponder that question.

1. Which of your students are committed to success?

2. Have you clearly defined what 'success' looks like?

3. How does that square with your students' definition of success?

4. Which of your teachers are committed to success?

5. Do you consider that all of the necessary people and resources in your school/system are aligned in order to be successful?

As you work to make your school what you'd like it to be and to meet the needs of your students in an equitable manner, you might want some deep reflection on commitment. I found that when I had questions like these, about the fundamental elements of school success, the more people we could get working on them, the better. As school leaders or teachers, we often feel like we have to have all of the answers. It's more productive to have good questions and to engage others in their exploration.

When you look across the landscape of your school, there is a noticeable behavioral difference between those who are committed, those who are involved, and the third group, those seeking to be invisible. (Category available for both students and faculty/staff) You can see this difference, and those who are involved/invisible require so much of your time, your energy, and your resources. My question to you is this: when you spend time with those individuals, what is on? Are you seeking to get them to commit?

Yes, we have kids in different grade-levels commit to graduating. That's a great idea and a nice vision piece. Now, work on gaining a commitment to the mission. What are the steps toward graduation? Let's make that into a commitment ceremony too. And, is graduation the thing you're seeking commitment for or A thing?

Committed individuals, given support, particularly from an accountability partner or a team approach, are more likely to reach the goals they seek than involved individuals who have a supervisor/teacher doing most of the heavy-lifting particularly in terms of commitment.

To have the school many of you are seeking, the pieces that

precede this one in the book lead you to the hardest but most important element of the school of excellence for every one... commitment.

If you could unlock commitment in the hearts and minds of ten percent more of your students/faculty, what would your school look like? Twenty percent? Thirty percent? There's a point where you'll reach critical mass and it's harder to stay out than it is to jump in.

To gain more committed individuals from the ranks of the involved, you'll need a deliberate, intentional strategy to connect students to conversations about their work, their dreams, their ideas, and help them have a short cycle plan of growth. And... we have to do it in a way that's not rushed and doesn't feel processed. It's usually true that it's not just what you do, but how you do it.

One other idea... work to move the invisible people up the continuum to the 'involved', or at least the 'uninvolved' list. To build a school of excellence for every one, you can't let students or teachers be invisible. Know people's names. Find out about their lives. Ask them what they're excited about. Move them from invisible and before you know it, you may be able to get them to commit to their own excellence.

Part III. Building Classrooms and Schools

for Every One and Everyone

There have been countless books written, hundreds of programs established, and billions of dollars spent in efforts to improve schools. From 70+ years in education (collectively not apiece!), we believe that at the core of any effort to improve school, there has to be a self-improvement effort on the part of those involved with the school. The change that you want to see has to begin with you first.

Change is an inside-out proposition. You want to change what you do? Begin by changing what you say. How do you do that? You change your thoughts. Your thoughts are influenced by your environment, so you have to choose your influences with intent, not chance. Good thoughts in- good thoughts out. You know what the greatest influence is on any teacher? The teachers in the rooms around her. We tend to behave like the people we spend the most time with. (Side bar: Middle school teachers spend a lot of time with middle school students...?!? :-)

We can build the classrooms/schools/systems we dream of when we can focus on the one and the one. Every one and everyone. There's something that can help you in this work: companions. It's hard to go about world-changing (or school-changing) on your own. Paradox—but the change has to begin inside of you. So, while you are working on you, you're also working with others. And your collective spirit will bolster your individual spirit. You become partners, a team, a group working toward something together.

We began this book with a focus on the individual side of the

'One' coin. We explored the collective side and the power of unity of purpose. In the first two sections we examined them separately. As we come together here in part three, we look at them together, working in union: one and one. Individual and collective. Because, as you work on you, you are able to more capably connect and collaborate with others... which strengthens you as an individual... and makes you a stronger member of the whole... over, and over, and over...

This is the part of the puzzle that makes it all work. When you begin to think in those terms. *That you are a part of this greater whole whose strength relies on your inner growth.* When you get to *there*, and you have others who arrive there too, you have moved from the *doing* stage to the *being* stage. I don't want to mislead you by saying "... and that's when it becomes easy..." because we are always influenced by other environmental factors (See "Global Pandemic, 2020-") and the context of the moment. We also are impacted by the passing of time and the need for continuous renewal (which requires an extraordinary level of commitment). If we have built our work driven by charismatic leaders instead of collaborative design, our progress can be upended or even worse, slip away.

BUT... when enough of you move from *doing to being,* things sort of get easy. We spend SO much time and energy in schools around *doing,* when we would create sustainable forces for good if we could focus on *being.* I know why... doing is more readily measured and more easily controlled. Being requires forces that you can't see that lead to changes that you can't help but see. That requires patience, and for no real or good reason, we keep going faster in what we do in schools, even on occasions when we're lost.

So many of the challenges we face would be so different if we pivoted from an *obsession with doing to a commitment about being*. For example: at the time of this writing, so many school people are struggling with students not doing their assignments during our current health crisis. When students are physically with us in the classroom, we are more likely to exert our will and control their actions. In other words, we can make them do the work when they are with us. For so many school leaders, that has led to an insistence to get children back to school. Yes, we all want all of the children who'd like to be in school to be there. But there's a point missed here: if we make students want to do assignments, we don't have to make them do them. If we focus on their *being*, and not their *doing* it would be that "teach someone to fish…" axiom, school-style. If we can help students to be *serious students expectant of quality work* rather than to *do work we expect them to do*, what might the results be?

And if you can see the doing/being conundrum among students, can you also see it for yourself? For teachers? When we *become* educators who are professional, collaborative, and committed, it's no longer about acting professionally, or doing collaboration, or choosing what is for the group and the greater good. When we *become* those educators, it is a matter of being. Then we continue on, works-in-progress, committed with other works-in-progress to the good of the whole and support for each other.

Building Classrooms for Every One and Everyone.

Capture. Inspire. Teach.

One of the most impactful educational experiences in my career was attending a summer program at the Child Development Center at Yale University. Conducted by Dr. James Comer, he taught us to understand the following:

> No significant teaching and learning can take shape in the absence of a significant relationship.

I have spent the last thirty-five years believing every word and applying it to my educational experiences at every level. Our educational experiences with our students and in our schools, shape and inform our work and purpose. As we continue to navigate the challenges we face daily, we must continue to draw upon, access, and activate the keys to success for our students. Dr. Comer's philosophy shaped my beliefs and at the core is an undeniable passion to see all students have hope for the future and pathways to reach and sustain that future.

I believe hope is a strategy, a belief and trust that something is possible. Through my varied educational experiences, there have been several on-ramps to deeper parts of my journey. Understanding the role positive relationships play in developing and sustaining student success has paved many bumpy roads. Moreover, relational trust developed between a teacher and student activates learning. I have discovered over time, there are three critical steps that lead to effective teaching and learning. Let's explore: Capture, Inspire, Teach.

1. Capture: Giving students a reason to learn;

2. Inspire: Giving students a reason to learn from you;

3. Teach: Permission is granted; student learning activated.

Teaching is one of the most important professions in the world... and one of the most difficult. Many in our field, as well as others, agree that today's students are unlike any generation before them, therefore, the emotional demands placed on teachers are at an unprecedented level. The experiences of this past year have reshaped views and changed the landscape of education. In this chapter, we want to offer the reader hope, inspiration and direction. Gone are the days of "educational experts" offering advice to school leaders and teachers without having the experience of being present and accounted for in a classroom or in a school with students.

Many of our teachers work in an environment that others would classify as tough, but yet, embrace the challenges of the demands placed upon them and meet success in spite of the odds. Throughout the pandemic and presently, educators all over the world have proven their worth. Further, they continue to defy the odds as they confront the unknowns of the future. Instead of returning to normal, we have an opportunity to enter into a new state of mindfulness where we begin to see things we didn't see before and understand the need to simplify the complexities of our work in order to advance it.

Capture, Inspire and Teach is a process designed to help teachers facilitate classrooms in a new era of teaching, while helping students cultivate new and exciting pathways to successful futures. This three-step process, anchored by solution-based instructional practices, is designed to drive both social-emotional and academic success in classrooms.

Pedagogically prescriptive, (CIT), provides the reader with specific strategies that can be implemented in classrooms anywhere. As a firm believer in the power of relationships, the foundation of this process exemplifies the work we all desire in our teachers at every level.

Having served as a superintendent of a school district, I see the need for a different type of professional development for our teachers. Our teachers need expertise in how to engage today's students in a positive learning environment.

I have witnessed with my own eyes, the *Capture, Inspire, and Teach* process transform even the "marginal teacher" into a teacher with the desire to become a "master teacher." We believe this is a journey worth taking. More importantly, it affirms and validates many of the practices we want to employ in our classrooms daily as we recognize the power of teaching and of being an active member of this incredible profession, the greatest of all time.

Understanding today's students is a prerequisite to teaching them. The more difficult they are to reach, the deeper the connection between teacher and student must be in order to create the right conditions for classroom success. My understanding of the students in my classroom evolved over time and produced energy I didn't know I possessed. As each year passed, the relationships developed with my students would prove invaluable. Many of the students I taught are still in contact with me and the experiences we have shared over the years confirm the need for educators to consciously engage in developing better practices that facilitate relational results in our classrooms and schools.

The background of this work began with my students teaching me before I had an opportunity to teach them. My top ten lessons learned from my students:

1. There was strength in numbers: there were more of them than there was of me.

2. They had a desire to learn, but not just anything.

3. They were disappointed with many of the adults in their lives.

4. They needed inspiration, hope and direction.

5. They were smart, but didn't want everyone to know how smart.

6. The tough exterior was a cover-up to a frightened child beneath.

7. They wanted a better life for themselves than the one they were living.

8. They wanted to know who I was and why in the world I would choose to become a teacher.

9. They would give me a chance if they felt I genuinely cared about them.

10. I needed their permission to teach them.

These lessons from my students also taught me that the foundation of successful classrooms and schools is not rooted in pedagogy; it is developed through positive relationships. While knowledge of subject matter is of critical importance, the connections we have with our students are equally critical. This is hard work, but more importantly, it's heart work.

Public education is facing its most critical times and one would find it difficult to argue with current statistical findings. I have come face to face with teachers and school leaders who actually are, as Teddy Roosevelt said, *"in the arena, whose faces are marred by dust, sweat and blood."* These interactions over time helped me understand and develop a renewed sense of hope for the future of our classrooms and schools. Moreover, seeing is believing, and observing some of the best teachers delivering highly skilled lessons to students considered by many to be "unteachable," led me back into public education and schools.

Regardless of our titles, we are all teachers. In our quest to be the best, we often stumble over simple processes that work. The *Capture, Inspire, and Teach* process was such a discovery as I struggled through my early years of teaching some of the students labeled "at-risk." Over the years, I, and many others have come to realize the majority of our students are "at-risk" in some category or regard. As such, we find ways to create conditions for success in our classrooms and schools. "CIT" is exactly that, a process that creates conditions for success for all students. As I struggled with some of my students, whether in my classroom as a teacher, an assistant principal as an administrator, a principal leading turn-around efforts, or even as a superintendent of a school district, I used this process as an approach that produced positive results over and over again.

As we continue to grasp and embrace the enormous responsibility of being a leader or a teacher of today's students, we must find constructive solutions to the complex issues we face daily. Office referrals in schools are increasing each year. (Peters, 2008) In large part, students appear angry with the adults in their lives who continue to disappoint them in one way or another. As we train our teachers to teach, it is difficult to find an undergraduate course, college, or university that prescriptively provides content preparation and behavioral solutions to such a magnitude of problems we face. Further, programs and processes of the past no longer solve today's problems in our school, classrooms, or communities.

Our education system directly affects our society, as our society affects our education system. The present status of both agencies demand change. However, change requires us to transform, think and react differently. For many, it's easier to remain the same. While some observers state, "our schools are broken," we say, they aren't broken, they are operating as designed.

Further, the organizational structures of our school systems and schools are no longer aligned with the realities our students face daily (Noguera,2015). Leaders and teachers who share the moral imperative to replace the traditional classroom with a modern or personalized learning environment must turn away from single-point solutions; instead, employ long-term, systemic solutions that help answer society's call to produce graduates with skills to compete in the industries of our time.

The future of education is in the hands of those who have the sustainable will and skill to fight the turbulent, unpredictable storm we face in our world of public education. As one of Georgia's finest administrators put it recently, "while acknowledging, we are all in this storm, we must also develop an understanding that we are in different boats."

Same storm — different boats

Understanding Influences on Our Students

The "typical" American family exists only in one's imagination. Sixty plus years ago, I was born into a family with a mother, father and five siblings. The youngest of six children, I grew up in a loving family. Our parents and the support system they had around them—grandmother, cousins, aunts, uncles, and close friends—formed a protective network and shielded us from adult problems and pressures. We were told, "school was our job and we couldn't afford to quit, get laid off or lose our job." As we Baby Boomers (most of whom were raised by both biological parents) came of age, the family structure in the 1970's suddenly collapsed in what demographers agree was the most dramatic change in family structure in American history (Putnam, 2015).

Those who have studied this change in family structure don't all agree on exactly what caused it, but most agree that these factors contributed:

- An individual swing of the cultural pendulum produced more emphasis on "self-fulfillment."
- The end of the long postwar boom began to reduce economic security for young working-class men.
- Millions of women, in part freed from norms, responded to new opportunities and headed to work.
- The feminist revolution transformed gender and marital norms. (Putnam, 2015).

The collapse of the traditional family hit the black community earliest and hardest, in part because that community was already clustered at the bottom of the economic hierarchy. During this period of seemingly anarchic change, it was possible to imagine that marriage and family were on their way to extinction. (Putnam,2015).

Carol Dweck (2006), a researcher at Stanford and author of *Mindset: The New Psychology of Success* discovered in her research that:

> ...belief guides a large part of your life. Much of what you think of as your personality actually grows out of this "mindset" and could prevent you from fulfilling your potential.

Further, you can have either a fixed mindset or a growth mindset. People are born with a love of learning, but the fixed mindset can undo it.

It can be confusing to some teachers and complex to many students, just because *some* people can accomplish a task with little or no training, that doesn't mean *others* couldn't also do it with adequate training. Learners with fixed mindsets about learning may be resistant to learning. If they believe they cannot do a math problem or read at a certain level, then they give up easily (Bray, McClaskey, 2015).

The process of "capturing a student" (Peters, 2008), facilitates a personalized learning environment. The teacher makes sure the student feels encouraged and knows he/she is there if and when needed. Trust is missing from the vocabulary and spirit of many of today's students as a result of some of the experiences they have encountered. Therefore, it is imperative that you note, in this three-step process "capture" is the first step.

At least a million illiterate students graduate from America's high schools each year. This means that these students cannot read, write, or use numbers sufficiently to get along in our society. From a recent study, 13% of 17-year-old students in our country are functionally illiterate; among minority students, the rate climbs to 40%.

The U.S. Department of Education estimates that our educational system has already left us with 24 million functional illiterates. These are not students who never went to school; these are students who, for the most part, have spent 8-12 years in our public schools (Thornburgh, 2006). When I became a principal in the early 90's, my staff and I began looking at our competition. We learned that we were not competing with other schools in our district or in other districts, but with the "home invasion" of our society. From our research, we identified five sources that strongly influenced children (in decreasing order of negative influence):

- Television/Media, to include video games and social media
- Peers
- Church
- School
- Home

We then developed a plan to combat or offset the power of the negative influences by moving from understanding the problems to creating solutions for all learners in our school. For many of us involved, it came down to remembering the major influences in our lives as children and how there was always a choice to be made. Unfortunately, many students today are making negative choices and receiving negative consequences as a result. Understanding our past is important because it allows us to understand the changes that have occurred, as well as their impact on society and our schools.

The influences listed above help us understand the multitude of needs our students have as they enter our schools and classrooms. Teachers receiving them are leaving the profession at an alarming rate due to the stress levels associated with attempting to educate them.

The process of Capturing, Inspiring and Teaching, is designed to take into consideration who our students are and why they are the way they are (identity), form trusting relationships with them (built on reciprocal respect) and inspire them to greater heights by teaching them in ways they've never been taught before.

Inspiration means: to fill someone with the urge or ability to do or feel something; to stimulate, motivate, encourage, influence, energize, incite. Many of us became teachers due to the influence of a former teacher or former teachers. It is a powerful experience to be inspired to the degree that it moves us to accomplish or achieve at the highest levels possible.

Teaching is one of the greatest professions that exist; a noble encounter with minds waiting to be captured and challenged. There is no better time than now for us to understand this dynamic phenomenon and respond with a level of tenacity that opens pathways of teaching and learning that do not presently exist; to forego best practices while developing better practices. Students that are "Captured and Inspired" will have opportunities unknown to them. As a teacher, I have experienced no better feeling than to see hope restored to a young person/student who had lost hope. We hold that power in our ability to understand, reason and respond with appropriate action to the forces against our learning institutions and children of whom we are called to teach.

Schools have not changed much in over one hundred years; someone from that period of time could walk into most schools today and feel right at home (Bray, McClaskey, 2015). Starting with "generation Y (1981-1996), education needed to change to keep students engaged. Since they grew up with technology, video games, and visuals that were coming at them faster with shorter segments, teachers found it difficult to keep their attention with traditional lectures. Many were forced to become entertainers in order to sustain even their best efforts. Schools attempted different approaches like whole language, cooperative learning. Project-based learning, and above all, added technology (Bray, McClaskey, 2015). Even with all these approaches/efforts, too many students were not paying attention, especially those that lived in poverty.

The third step in the CIT process is to Teach. It is important to understand when students have a voice and choice in their own learning, teachers change the way they teach. This results in the learner taking more responsibility and ownership of their learning. Further, one might pay close attention to the fact that teaching is the third step, not the first. Teaching is defined as, "the occupation, profession, or work of a teacher; the ideas or principles taught by an authority." For many years, teachers repeated the same process and used the same materials to teach different groups of students. As mentioned earlier, we must also take into consideration the difference in students of the past and present-day ones. Teachers who seek mastery need challenges in order to stay motivated (Jackson, 2013). Jackson states, "master teachers do not need to rehearse the same skills over and over; they need to continue to be mindful as they teach."

As we address the third step in this three-step process of effective teaching and learning, it is imperative that we stress the importance of reflection. Students, on the other hand, are concerned about a variety of things.

In my research for the work surrounding my book, "Do You Know Enough About Me to Teach Me," we interviewed many students who shared their "discontent" with what and how their teachers taught. In addition, they were "turned-off" to the learning opportunities because of how the information was presented. For more than thirty years, the notion that teaching methods should match a learner's particular learning style has had a powerful influence on education. (Bray, McClaskey, 2015). One important implication of this research is that skills acquired early in childhood are foundational and make later learning more efficient. Thus, experiences in those years are especially significant (Putnam, 2015). As we teach today's students, we must take note of the fact that intellectual and socio-emotional development are intertwined from an early age. Further, a child's interaction with positive, caring, and responsive adults is essential to creating the right conditions for success in any classroom.

The problems our schools are encountering are complex and dependent on multiple, interrelated solutions that address the core of the issues our students bring to school each day. It is often more challenging to establish a shared classroom vision when we face constant resistance from multiple sources. Another challenge is providing professional learning that prepares teachers to perform in a modern setting while keeping pace with the demands placed upon them.

Often, these demands have little to do with establishing positive relationships with students, but more with placing a label upon them. Adherence to traditional teaching methods prevents teachers and students from leveraging their full capability, such as the ability to personalize or individualize learning. Information is needed to personalize learning; does this student prefer working alone or in groups, does he/she feel comfortable being the spokesperson or work behind the scenes, is student an independent worker or doe he/she need to be encouraged to do more, do my students like the set-up of our classroom or would they like to change it to better suit their arrangement choice? These questions are essential to developing the relationship that should be a prerequisite in any effective teacher's classroom.

Expectations Determine the Possibilities of Every Classroom

Nobody Rises to Low Expectations.

The classroom philosophy should be based on the fact that students naturally want to learn the skills needed to grow into capable adults. Further, they want to be free to choose how they will become successful. The freedom to choose how their classroom operates, how they will spend their time and exert their energy, builds personal responsibility. Our students progress at their own pace with the teacher serving as facilitator.

Throughout the "capture, inspire, teach" process, there should be multiple opportunities over time to demonstrate what a student knows and is able to do at any given time and at what level. When principals and teachers exhibit high expectations and concern and serve as appropriate role models, they help militate against the likelihood of academic failure, particularly for students in difficult life circumstances. In order for educators to build productive relationships and connections with students, it is important to understand what is going on in students' lives away from school.

Close relationships with teachers and others in the school can reduce stress and provide positive support throughout difficult times. Educators can not only provide instructional support for academic content and skills, but also serve as confidants and internal support for students. Highly effective teachers help their students develop values and attitudes needed to persevere and excel in their schoolwork. They introduce new, meaningful and relevant experiences that make learning interesting to today's students. The most important thing educators can do is to promote educational resilience by encouraging students to master new experiences, believe in their own efficacy, and take responsibility for their own learning.

We know now that all students, including those with special needs, can surpass high academic standards when provided with relevant and stimulating content and instruction, as well as support, tailored to their individual strengths and learning needs. By contrast, information and subject matter that are disconnected from students' experiences, culture, and needs contribute to their learning problems and ultimately their failure to connect and lack of desire to do so.

It is important to remember that the school, family, or the community acting alone cannot address the multiple risks and adversities that today's generation of students face. Rather, the resources within these three contexts must be harnessed if educators are to solve the educational, psychological, and social issues that confront families and our students. Our students are bright, resilient, eager, and curious, and all have the ability and desire to learn; the problem is reaching out to them in ways that engage and encourage them.

Researchers using an action research design conducted a series of intervention studies on how schools can be more responsive to today's students by changing their organization and using innovative approaches to service delivery. These studies focused on the areas of (1) implementing small unit organization to improve student engagement, (2) collegiality among staff, and (3) cross-disciplinary collaboration (Oxley, 1994). Findings suggest the importance of the following:

- Changing the mind-set of administrators and the teaching staff on how learning takes place.
- Implementation of coordinated approaches to organizing school resources.
- Staff development that focuses on developing strategies and expertise for meeting the diverse needs of students.

In several schools studied, these changes were found to produce significant improvements in teachers' attitudes toward school and ability to institute radical changes in the service of students, as well as enhanced student motivation and improved student achievement (Nash, n.d.). School districts and schools are finding themselves in a precarious position, serving both as a delivery system to their students and as the foundation for the delivery to take place.

In order to increase our chances of delivering quality to our students and school communities, we must remember, quality is never an accident; it is the result of careful planning and skillful execution. The capture, inspire, teach process covered in this chapter is the wisest choice of many alternatives when it comes to effectives ways to teach this generation of learners. Further, it grants us the license to teach.

You can't have schools for every one and everyone without

having classrooms that achieve the same. Those classrooms are made more intentional with the approach of Capture, Inspire and Teach. That relational model, fortified with high expectations for every one, leads to classroom success that spreads across the entire school.

Building Schools for Every One and Everyone.

One Morgan.

Dexter Mills was the head of School Improvement for the Georgia Department of Education, and he had a keen eye for innovators and innovative schools. His vision was to identify sites as models and exemplars for other school leaders to visit, to study, and to gain successful practices from.

At Morgan County High School, we were honored to be selected as one of the five *Secondary Redesign Schools*, sharing the creative work of our teachers and students with other school people from across the state. Barbara Bishop was our consultant from GADOE in the process, and one of her roles was to help collect the data and details of what we were doing differently at MCHS in order to share with others. Barbara deserves credit for a lot of things but specifically two that helped build our culture at Morgan.

You have a student handbook, right? Barbara suggested (and then served as editor and producer) that we capture the essence of what we were doing at MCHS and include it in a document that was less handbook-y and more like a magazine. Our first edition of *Pursuits* was born, with these sections: who we are; what we believe; how we do what we do. Incorporating our values into this piece was more important than even *we* thought at the time. If you are indeed driven by your values, you ought to talk about them frequently. Build your processes around them. Not just laminate them.

Pursuits became an annual full-color, around 100-page, everything-about-MCHS magazine that we shared with students and families, but also around our community. Waiting in the doctor's office? There's a copy of *Pursuits* in the lobby. Visiting a local hotel? There's *Pursuits* as you are waiting to get checked in. Getting your car worked on? How about taking a look at our school's programs in a copy of *Pursuits*?

Someone's going to tell your story, and it might as well be you. And if you are going to tell your school's story, color photos of your students and teachers in action speak thousands of words.

Barbara gave us a great gift with her idea for *Pursuits*, but an even bigger contribution came from a phrase she had placed in one of the pages. Remember, Barbara worked for the Georgia Department of Education so she was able to come in from outside, and take a look on the inside, so she was there as a scientist, and observer, and she could see things that those of us working there might not so easily see. In her assessment of what we did, and who we were, she summed it up in this well-known phrase:

E Pluribus Unum.

From many, one.

The motto of the United States of America, and a phrase Barbara included in the first (of many) editions of *Pursuits*.

It's amazing how the frequency of seeing something etches it into your mind. That phrase was not only included in *Pursuits*, it was on the back cover. That back cover was something that I saw... well, everywhere. (Remember, we printed a bunch of these and spread them out all over Morgan County) It was also our student handbook, so it was a document (although it felt and looked like a magazine) that we referred to daily in our work. And day after day, that phrase kept finding its way into my brain.

Fast Forward. It's the spring of the following year, and a local civic organization is hosting a talent show at our school to raise funds for scholarships for MCHS students. A worthwhile cause indeed.

The event itself is completely directed and operated by the civic club; it wasn't a school event, even though it targeted our students for both performers and for audience members. So, it's our students, at our school, but not operated by us, or operated in the *manner* we would do so.

No offense intended to the nice folks at the civic club working to raise funds for scholarships for our students: it's just that *their vision of students and our vision of students were very different*. At the event itself, they had people at each door making sure no one slipped into the auditorium without first going to the ticket stand. That's not a bad thing by itself, but it created an optic, an image that our students weren't used to. We prided ourselves on being a school of *responsible freedoms* so we didn't have adults hovering over students at assemblies. We worked to *teach* the behaviors we expected and *discuss* needed adjustments when necessary, but to provide an environment that was as open and inviting as we could.

The civic club had not been with us along the way for our transformation, so they behaved like they remembered school being, and not like we operated it. So, the comfortable, safe environment our students were used to was replaced by a much different one, but again, it's in our building, with our students, so our students found it unexpectedly.

We had a trio scheduled to perform. Shelby McLeod (an amazing singer who later went on to perform in Nashville, among many other accolades), art teacher, musician and all-around supporter Ty Manning, and Richard Thomas (aka "Dicky T") on percussion. They planned to perform a version of KT Tunstall's *Black Horse and the Cherry Tree*. I was seated in the auditorium (as a support of our kids, not as the supervisor of the event) and in the row behind me were members of Dicky T's family. Lots of family members. Right before the show started, Richard joined them, and I came to know that he'd been told he couldn't perform, that he'd missed a mandatory dress rehearsal the night before (he'd been at a high school band event, so…) and that he couldn't be in the talent show.

Now, Dicky T was there to help out a friend, to provide accompaniment, but the people wouldn't let him play. And all of his family was there. They all were very gracious.

Our students involved in the event were angry.

That evening, one after another of them came to me and told me that what happened wasn't right. That they should've let Dicky T play. I asked them this: *what are you going to do about it?*

What happened next became the driving force for our school and much of its success for the next decade plus.

A group of students came to see me the next morning to share their frustration about what had gone down and how things had happened.

"Those people don't know how we do things here," one of the students said. "We don't let each other down like that," said another. "That's not how we are here. We're *one* here... we don't do that."

So, I asked again, "what are you going to do about it?"

Here's what they did. They put on their *own* concert. And it wasn't a talent show, because they wanted to cheer for each other and support each other. And it wasn't going to have some adult host that didn't know the students. In fact, no host at all. In fact, no adults (at least out front).

Our students put on their *own* show, their *own* way, with their *own* purpose and direction.

They asked the Culinary Arts department to do concessions. They got Future Business Leaders to handle the money (which they shifted to a donation rather than a charge *so everyone could come if they wanted)*. The Tech kids set up cameras and displayed close ups via projector on the walls. Ever been to a concert? This was like that. Ever watched the Grammys where they connect performers from different genres of music? Yeah, that's what our kids did. Our all-star rapper and country diva singing together? Yep, that happened.

See, it wasn't just about doing it their way: it was that *their* way was all about *coming together as one. From many, one.* **One Morgan.**

Their concert was billed as "One Morgan: The Concert," and from that moment was born our movement. It became our mantra. It was not just a slogan we said, but also the way we lived. It was our way of doing school. It worked (and at the time of this writing, even though I've been gone from the school for some time, it's still going strong) because we lived it enough to say it, and we said it enough after that to help us live it more strongly.

One Morgan, from that birth, became the symbol of our school and eventually our entire school system, and later on our county. (When the County's leaders made a video about COVID-19 safety, it ended with each of them saying "One Morgan.") When our basketball team took the state championship, the headline in the local paper was *"Won Morgan!"*

It's a phrase that unites people, but it's more than that.

Through ongoing conversations about what it is and what it isn't, from our interrogation of it as a value when we didn't live up to its potential, through asking our students and teachers to talk about it, to write about it, we helped refine the notion of One... that every one, like Dicky T, percussionist, matters, and the everyone coming together to work towards each other's success is a way of living that is self-fulfilling. (Side note... Dicky T was the house band drummer for the *One Morgan* Concert)

Like anything that sets the beat for others to move to, *One Morgan* was something we built... not in one concert, not in a day, but over time. It's a simple proposition... let's all support each other and find joy in each other's triumphs. And, let's not miss anybody... let's think about others and what they may need. Collectively, we make sure that every individual is valued, and respected, and listened to, and appreciated. Individually, we do our part to support that collective, to be a part of the good and kind spirit that Dostoyevsky speaks of in *The Brothers Karamazov:*

> And even though we may be involved with the most important affairs, achieve distinction or fall into some great misfortune—all the same, let us never forget how good we all once felt here, all together, *united by such good and kind feelings as made us, too,...perhaps better than we actually are* (emphasis added).

One.

References

Berger, W. (2014). *A More Beautiful Question: The Power of Inquiry to Spark Breakthrough Ideas* (0 ed.). Bloomsbury USA.

Colburn, L., & Beggs, L. (2020). *The Wraparound Guide*. Amsterdam University Press.

Cole, J., & Degen, B. (2001). *The Magic School Bus Explores the Senses*. Scholastic.

Comer, J. P., Haynes, N. M., Joyner, E. T., & Ben-Avie, M. (1996). *Rallying the Whole Village*. Amsterdam University Press.

de Saint-Exupéry, A., & Howard, R. (2000). *The Little Prince*. (1st ed.). Mariner Books.

Dostoyevsky, F. *The Brothers Karamazov*. (2002). Farrar, Straus and Giroux.

Dunn R., & Dunn, K. (1993). *Teaching secondary students through their individual learning styles: Practical approaches for grades 7-12*. Boston, MA: Allyn & Bacon.

Flippen, F. (2008). *The Flip Side*. Van Haren Publishing.

Kosovich, Jeff & Hulleman, Chris & Barron, Kenneth. (2017). Measuring Motivation in Educational Settings: A Case for Pragmatic Measurement.

Mack, Julie. jmack1@mlive.com. (2010, July 6). *Changing schools can be hard on children academically and socially*. Mlive. https://www.mlive.com/opinion/kalamazoo/2010/07/changing_schools_can_be_hard_o.html

Mathers, M. (2002). Lose Yourself [CD]. United States: 8 Mile: Music From and Inspired By The Motion Picture.

Peters, S.G. (2007). *Teaching to capture and inspire all learners: Bringing your best stuff everyday*. Thousand Oaks, CA: Corwin Press.

Peters, S.G. (2006). *Do you know enough about me to teach me?* Second edition, expanded version. Orangeburg, SC: The Peters Group Foundation.

Rumberger, R. W. (2011). *Dropping Out: Why Students Drop Out of High School and What Can Be Done About It*. Harvard University Press.

Scott, S. (2004). *Fierce Conversations: Achieving Success at Work and in Life One Conversation at a Time* (Reprint ed.). Berkley.

Sinek, S. (2009). *Start with Why: How Great Leaders Inspire Everyone to Take Action* (Illustrated ed.). Portfolio.

Taylor, B. J. (2021). *Whole Brain Living: The Anatomy of Choice and the Four Characters That Drive Our Life*. Hay House Inc.

Tinto, V. (1997). Classrooms as communities: Exploring the educational character of student persistence. *Journal of Higher Education*, 68, 599-623.

Wilson, B., & Cole, P. (1996), *Cognitive teaching models*. In D. H. Jonassen (Ed.), Handbook of research for educational communications and technology (pp. 601-621). New York, NY: MacMillan.